SECOND REVISED EDITION

# Writer's Workshop

## *A Self-Paced Program for Composition Mastery*

**Robert Frew**
**Richard Guches**
**Robert Mehaffy**

*American River College*
*Sacramento, California*

*Illustrated by Barbara Coulson Clark*

Peek Publications · Box 11065 · Palo Alto, California 94306

ISBN 0-917962-43-5

Manufactured in the United States of America

# *Preface*

*Writer's Workshop* is designed to review principles that you learned previously and to teach you new concepts and skills. To make your work easier, you should read the objectives listed for each unit before you do the exercises in the unit. That way you will understand what skills and concepts are to be learned prior to the unit's posttest. Furthermore, you should notice that an understanding of the objectives will make clear the purpose of each exercise. With this understanding, you can work through the unit and its exercises as rapidly as you are able. Wherever possible exercise answers are supplied so that you may rapidly see whether or not you understand the instruction. Where the answers are not given in the book, you should have your work checked as soon as possible so that you may review or restudy to correct misconceptions.

Also, you should use the many student-written examples as models to follow. These can help you write the exercises, pretests, and practice tests that are designed to prepare you for the unit posttests. Almost every example in *Writer's Workshop* was written by a student.

Whether reviewing or learning a new idea, make certain that you understand the objectives and that you have mastered the skills before you are asked to demonstrate that mastery on unit posttests. Work as fast as you are able to but as slowly as you need to; like learning to type or to play tennis, once you have mastered the basics, you must practice and practice and practice to become truly skillful.

# Contents

# UNIT ONE
# Simple Sentences: Punctuation Principles

## Objectives

After completing this unit, you will be able to

1. divide a *simple sentence* into its *complete subject* and *complete predicate*.
2. identify the *simple subject* and *simple predicate* in a simple sentence.
3. write the following kinds of simple sentences:
    —one in which the *subject does something,*
    —one in which *something happens to the subject,*
    —one in which the *complete predicate tells what condition the subject is in,*
    —one in which the *complete predicate tells who or what the subject is,*
    —one with a *verb phrase* for a simple predicate,
    —a *question,*
    —a *command,*
    —an *inverted sentence,*
    —one in which an **-ing** *verb functions as the simple subject.*
4. identify *compound subjects* and *compound predicates* in simple sentences.
5. write simple sentences with *compound subjects* and *compound predicates.*
6. use *commas* to set off *introductory words and phrases.*
7. use *commas* to separate *adjacent words and word groups.*
8. use *commas* to enclose *words and phrases that interrupt sentences.*
9. use *commas* to separate *words and phrases at the ends of sentences.*

**1**

# Unit One Pretest

Before you begin the lessons in Unit One, your instructor may want you to take this pretest to discover whether you need to concentrate on Lesson One, Lesson Two, or both lessons.

You can check many of the items yourself by turning to the ANSWERS ON PAGE 6. *Your instructor must check items 13-20*

| **Passing Scores** | **Your Scores** |
|---|---|
| Part One - 54 points | Part One - _____ points (60 pts. possible) |
| Part Two - 36 points | Part Two - _____ points (40 pts. possible) |

**PART ONE: LESSON ONE (3 points each sentence)**

**Directions:**

Place a slash mark (/) between the *complete subject* and the *complete predicate* in each of the following sentences.

1. The winters on Grey Mountain are brutal.
2. Sharon Bidwell's sister is a certified public accountant.
3. Three people in the company knew the identity of the embezzler.
4. His plans to restore the windmill had been ruined by the storm.

**Directions:**

Identify the *simple subject* and *simple predicate* in each of the following sentences.

| **SIMPLE SUBJECT** | **SIMPLE PREDICATE** | |
|---|---|---|
| _____ | _____ | 5. Harold's friend gave them a ride to the airport. |
| _____ | _____ | 6. The set of Japanese chests looks very old. |
| _____ | _____ | 7. Wait five more minutes. |
| _____ | _____ | 8. But his reasons for leaving the job Carol could understand. |

**Directions:**

If a sentence has a *simple* subject or predicate, write *SIMPLE* in the appropriate blank. If the sentence has a *compound* subject or predicate, write *COMPOUND* in the appropriate blank.

| **SUBJECT** | **PREDICATE** | |
|---|---|---|
| _____ | _____ | 9. The passengers screamed and yelled at the customs men. |
| _____ | _____ | 10. The trip to New York was short and hectic. |
| _____ | _____ | 11. Jean and Frank work well together but fight constantly at home. |
| _____ | _____ | 12. Lionel fought for the United States in Vietnam and then became a mercenary in an African civil war. |

**3**

**Directions:**

Write the kind of *simple sentence* requested.

13. Write a *simple sentence* in which the *subject does something.*

_____

_____

14. Write a *simple sentence* in which *something happens to the subject.*

_____

_____

15. Write a *simple sentence* in which the *complete predicate tells what condition the subject is in.*

_____

_____

16. Write a *simple sentence* in which the *complete predicate tells who or what the subject is.*

_____

_____

**Directions:**

Write one of each kind of *simple* sentence as directed.

17. Simple subject and compound predicate.

_____

_____

18. Simple subject and simple predicate

_____

_____

19. Compound subject and compound predicate.

_____

**4** _____

20. Compound subject and simple predicate.

_____

_____

**PART TWO: LESSON TWO** (4 points each sentence)

**Directions:**

Insert *commas* where they are needed in the following sentences. If a sentence needs no commas, write *C* in the left-hand margin.

21. However the passengers near the rear door of the plane were able to escape.
22. Bill an avid fan of the Dodgers bought a season's ticket.
23. During a visit to Vancouver three years ago it rained and rained and rained.
24. The frightened horse to make matters worse stepped on the fallen rider.
25. Mary thinking she was late for work ran out of the front door and found the Sunday paper on the front porch.
26. Excited by the prospect of being a professional model she daydreamed about magazine ads and television commercials.
27. The crew was well trained disciplined and determined to win.
28. Sue was a tall slim girl with long black hair.
29. The Highway Commission will soon begin hearings on the proposed freeway fee a tax violently opposed by the state automobile dealers.
30. With the profits from her investments in real estate and restaurant franchises Norma was able to build a beautiful home at Lake Tahoe.

**Answers for Unit One Pretest**

1. The winters on Grey Mountain / are brutal.
2. Sharon Bidwell's sister / is a certified public accountant.
3. Three people in the company / knew the identity of the embezzler.
4. His plans to restore the windmill / had been ruined by the storm.
5. friend          gave
6. set             looks
7. [You]         Wait
8. Carol        could understand
9. SIMPLE       COMPOUND
10. SIMPLE      SIMPLE
11. COMPOUND    COMPOUND
12. SIMPLE      COMPOUND

13-20. Have your instructor check these sentences.

21. However , the passengers near the rear door of the plane were able to escape.
22. Bill , an avid fan of the Dodgers , bought a season's ticket.
23. During a visit to Vancouver three years ago , it rained and rained and rained.
24. The frightened horse , to make matters worse , stepped on the fallen rider.
25. Mary , thinking she was late for work , ran out of the front door and found the Sunday paper on the front porch.
26. Excited by the prospect of being a professional model , she daydreamed about magazine ads and television commercials.
27. The crew was well trained , disciplined , and determined to win.

*or*

The crew was well trained , disciplined and determined to win.

28. C or Sue was a tall , slim girl with long , black hair.
29. The Highway Commission will soon begin hearings on the proposed freeway fee , a tax violently opposed by the state automobile dealers.
30. With the profits from her investments in real estate and restaurant franchises , Norma was able to build a beautiful home at Lake Tahoe.

# 1

## LESSON ONE—Writing Simple Sentences

### Complete Subjects and Complete Predicates

The basic sentence in English composition is the *simple sentence*. Usually a simple sentence contains a *subject* that is followed by a *predicate*. The topic of a sentence—who or what is being written about—is the *complete subject* of the sentence. What is told about the subject is *the complete predicate* of the sentence. You should be able to identify the subject and predicate in any sentence you write.

### Who or What Does What?

Often a sentence can be divided into its complete subject and complete predicate by asking *who* or *what does what?* By asking **who** or **what** does what, you can find the *subject* being written about; by asking what does the subject **do**, you can locate the *predicate*.

*Examples*

| COMPLETE SUBJECT (Who or What?) | COMPLETE PREDICATE (Does What?) |
|---|---|
| 1. Piranhas | bite. |
| 2. The hairy, foamy-mouthed monster | loved the beautiful young maiden. |

7

### What Happens to the Subject?

Sometimes, however, the complete predicate answers the question, *what happens to the subject?*

*Examples*

|  COMPLETE SUBJECT<br>(Who or What?) | COMPLETE PREDICATE<br>(What Happens to the Subject?) |
|---|---|
| 1. The books | have been returned to the library. |
| 2. The deer | were often seen in the meadow at dusk. |
| 3. The new design of Carl's | will be tested many times. |

### What Is the Subject's Condition?

At other times the complete predicate tells *what condition the subject is, was, or will be in*—the subject's state of being.

*Examples*

|  COMPLETE SUBJECT<br>(Who or What?) | COMPLETE PREDICATE<br>(Conditions of Subject?) |
|---|---|
| 1. The avocado | is soft. |
| 2. The clerk in the Housewares department | looked exhausted at the end of the sale. |
| 3. The drink | will be very refreshing. |

**8** In what condition is the *avocado*? What is its state of being? What kind of avocado is it? It is **soft**. It is a soft avocado.

Adjective   Noun
a **soft**   avocado

What condition was the *clerk* in: what was his state of being? What kind of clerk was he: a **well-rested** *clerk*? a **friendly** *clerk*? a very **helpful** *clerk*? How did he *look*? He *looked* **exhausted.**

Adjective    Noun
the **exhausted** *clerk*

What will be the condition of the *drink*? What kind of a drink will it be? It will be a **refreshing** *drink*.

Adjective    Noun
a **refreshing** *drink*

---

**Adjectives**

*Adjectives* are words that modify (change or alter the meaning of) *nouns* or *pronouns*.
ADJ   N     ADJ   N   ADJ   N     ADJ   N    PRO   V    ADJ    PRO   V   ADJ
*big* man/   *small* man   *red* paint/   *yellow* paint   She was *foolish*/   She was *wise*.

---

**Who Or What Is the Subject?**

The complete predicate may also tell *who* or *what* the subject is, was, or will be. The subject is *who*? A complete predicate that answers this question renames or identifies the subject.

*Examples*

| COMPLETE SUBJECT<br>(Who or What?) | COMPLETE PREDICATE<br>(The Subject is Who?) |
|---|---|
| 1. Our teacher | is a photographer. |
| 2. The reduced price | seems to be a real bargain. |
| 3. The pilots | were experienced combat flyers. |
| 4. Ugly caterpillars | become pretty butterflies. |

The *teacher* and the **photographer** are the same person. The noun **photographer** is another name for the *teacher*.

noun that renames
*teacher* = **photographer**

The reduced *price* seems to be a **bargain.** In other words, the *price* is a **bargain.**

noun that renames
*price* = **bargain**

Who were the *pilots*? They were experienced combat **flyers.**

noun that renames
*pilots* = **flyers**

**9**

What do ugly *caterpillars* become? They become pretty **butterflies.**

noun that renames
*Caterpillars* = **butterflies**

**EXERCISE 1**

Place a slash mark (/) between the *complete subject* and the *complete predicate*. (Answers on page 34)

1. The subway train rolled to a stop.
2. He should have waited for the rain to stop.
3. A stubborn high-pressure ridge kept the winter rains away from the West Coast.
4. The worst time of year for some people is Christmas.
5. She bought her boyfriend a gold ring for his birthday.

### Simple Subjects and Simple Predicates

The **simple subject** in any sentence is the subject after all of the modifying words and word groups (adjectives, adverbs, prepositional phrases, etc.) have been removed. The simple subject is usually a noun or pronoun.

*Examples*

| COMPLETE SUBJECTS | SIMPLE SUBJECTS |
|---|---|
| 1. *Piranhas* | Piranhas (*noun*) |
| 2. The hairy, foamy-mouthed *monster* | monster (*noun*) |
| 3. The *books* | books (*noun*) |
| 4. The new *design* of Carl's | design (*noun*) |
| 5. The *clerk* in the Housewares department | clerk (*noun*) |
| 6. *They* | They (*pronoun*) |

The **simple predicate** of a sentence is the central verb—*the key verb*—in the complete predicate. This verb may be accompanied by helping verbs.

| SOME HELPING VERBS | | | | | | | |
|---|---|---|---|---|---|---|---|
| am | are | is | was | were | be | been | being |
| have | has | had | having | | | | |
| do | does | did | done | doing | | | |
| can | must | | | | | | |
| about to | keep on | to be | to + verb | | | | |

**10**

A verb accompanied by helping verbs is called a *verb phrase.*

*Examples*

1. is going
2. have known
3. to wonder
4. are being built
5. will have finished

The *simple predicate* is the key verb, or verb phrase, stripped of all its objects and its modifying words.

*Examples*

| COMPLETE SUBJECT | COMPLETE PREDICATE | SIMPLE PREDICATE |
|---|---|---|
| 1. Big Sur Sally | *soaked* in her redwood hot-tub every evening. | soaked |
| 2. The four scientists | *had worked* on the formula for ten years. | had worked |
| 3. John | *is buying* new tires for his car. | is buying |

The simple subjects and simple predicates are more difficult to find in other kinds of sentences:

## Commands

In **commands** the simple subject is the pronoun *you,* in spite of the fact that the "you" is not stated in the sentence.

*Examples*

| UNSTATED SIMPLE SUBJECT | SIMPLE PREDICATE | |
|---|---|---|
| 1. [You] | *Quiet* | down, now! |
| 2. [You] | *Take* | the third seat in row four. |
| 3. [You] | *Buckle* | your seat belts please. |

## Questions

The simple subject and simple predicate may be harder to find in a **question** if the simple predicate is a *verb phrase* (a verb with helping verbs in front of it) and part of the phrase comes before the subject.

*Examples*

| HELPING VERB | SIMPLE SUBJECT | HELPING VERB | VERB |
|---|---|---|---|
| 1. **Is** | *she* | | **working** today? |
| 2. **Should** | *they* | **have** | **bought** the house? |
| 3. **Did** | *he* | **get** | **mugged** in the parking lot again? |

*The simple subject may be hard to find.*

The simple subject may also be hard to find in *questions* that begin with words such as the following:

| | | |
|---|---|---|
| who | whom | whomever |
| which | where | whichever |
| what | whatever | |
| when | whenever | |
| where | wherever | |
| how | however | |
| why | why . . . ever | |

*Examples*

| | SIMPLE SUBJECT | SIMPLE PREDICATE | |
|---|---|---|---|
| 1. | *Who* | has | the time? |

| | | SIMPLE SUBJECT | SIMPLE PREDICATE | |
|---|---|---|---|---|
| 2. | *Which* | room | will be | available? |

| | | HELPING VERB | SIMPLE SUBJECT | VERB |
|---|---|---|---|---|
| 3. | *Where* | will | they | eat? |

The verb phrase *will eat* is the simple predicate.

## Inverted Sentences

In a typical sentence the subject precedes the predicate, but in an **inverted sentence** the word order is changed so that the predicate, or part of it, is placed before the subject.

*Examples*

**12**

| | | SIMPLE SUBJECT | | SIMPLE PREDICATE | |
|---|---|---|---|---|---|
| 1. | My | *love* | | **is** | true. (typical) |

| | SIMPLE PREDICATE | | SIMPLE SUBJECT | |
|---|---|---|---|---|
| True | **is** | | my | *love.* (inverted) |

|  | SIMPLE SUBJECT | SIMPLE PREDICATE | |
|---|---|---|---|
| 2. | *I* | **can do** | without his criticism. (typical) |

|  | | SIMPLE SUBJECT | SIMPLE PREDICATE | |
|---|---|---|---|---|
| His criticism | | *I* | **can do** | without. (inverted) |

### There Is, Here Is

In sentences that begin "*There is*" and "*Here is*," the subject always comes *after* the predicate. The word *there* or *here* is never the subject. (This type of sentence is more acceptable in conversation than academic writing. Use this type of sentence sparingly, or better yet, not at all.)

*Examples*

|  | | SIMPLE PREDICATE | | SIMPLE SUBJECT | | |
|---|---|---|---|---|---|---|
| 1. There | | **is** | | *Helen.* | | |
| 2. There | | **is** | a | *leak* | | in the car's cooling system. |
| 3. Here | | **is** | the best | *way* | | to work this problem. |

### -Ing Verbs Used As Subject

A *verb* ending with an *-ing* may function as the simple subject of a sentence.

*Examples*

|  | SIMPLE SUBJECT | | SIMPLE PREDICATE | | |
|---|---|---|---|---|---|
| 1. | **Skiing** | in the Sierras | *was delayed* | | by the lack of snow. |
| 2. Her | **writing** | | *is* | | the great joy of her life. |

## EXERCISE 2

Identify the *simple subject* and *simple predicate* in each of the following sentences. (Answers on page 34)

| SIMPLE SUBJECT | SIMPLE PREDICATE | |
|---|---|---|
| _____ | _____ | 1. The horned owl glided over the rooftops of the subdivision. |
| _____ | _____ | 2. The boat on the horizon was a schooner from Boston. |
| _____ | _____ | 3. The grass had been piled in the street. |
| _____ | _____ | 4. The battery was very weak. |

_____ _____    5. When will the second movie begin?

_____ _____    6. There is no safe place in the city.

_____ _____    7. Stay until five o'clock.

_____ _____    8. Hang-gliding is not a sport for the timid.

_____ _____    9. His motive for resigning no one could understand.

_____ _____   10. The first woman to successfully climb the mountain had never received much publicity for her feat.

## EXERCISE 3

Write the kind of *simple sentence* requested.

1. Write a **simple sentence** in which the *subject does something*.

_____

_____

_____

2. Write a **simple sentence** in which *something happens to the subject.*

_____

_____

3. Write a **simple sentence** in which the *complete predicate tells what condition the subject is in.*

_____

_____

4. Write a **simple sentence** in which the *complete predicate tells who or what the subject is.*

_____

**14**

_____

5. Write a **simple sentence** with a *verb phrase* for a *simple predicate.*

_____

_____

_____

6. Write a **question.**

_____

_____

_____

7. Write a **command.**

_____

_____

_____

8. Write an **inverted sentence.**

_____

_____

_____

9. Write a **simple sentence** that begins with "*There is*" or "*Here is.*"

_____

_____

_____

(Do not use this kind of sentence very often in your writing.)

10. Write a **simple sentence** in which an *-ing verb functions as the simple subject.*

_____

_____

_____

Have your sentences checked.

## Compound Subjects and Predicates

### Compound Subjects

One type of sentence that frequently creates difficulties for the beginning writer is the *simple sentence* with a **compound subject**. In this kind of sentence, the writer says something about two or more things or people.

|  | SIMPLE SUBJECT #1 | | SIMPLE SUBJECT #2 | SIMPLE PREDICATE | |
|---|---|---|---|---|---|
| 1. | *Frankie* | and | *Johnnie* | **were** | lovers. |

SIMPLE SUBJECT #1

2. The Kennedy Marching *Band* from Cleveland and the Regimental Drum and

SIMPLE SUBJECT #2    SIMPLE PREDICATE

Bugle *Corps* **marched** together

in the Saint Patrick's Day parade.

In each of the sentences above, two subjects have something in common. Because of the relationship between the subjects in each sentence, only one predicate is needed to make a statement about both subjects. Even though each sentence has more than one subject, it is a simple sentence because each contains just one simple predicate.

### Compound Predicates

The *simple sentence* with **compound predicate** is used frequently. In this type of simple sentence, two or more predicates work together to make a statement about the subject of the sentence.

|  | SIMPLE SUBJECT | SIMPLE PREDICATE #1 | | SIMPLE PREDICATE #2 |
|---|---|---|---|---|
| 1. | *Dogs* | **bark** | and | **bite.** |

SIMPLE SUBJECT    SIMPLE PREDICATE #1

2. The *ferryboat* **gained** some time on the trip to Tiburon but

SIMPLE PREDICATE #2

**lost** it on the trip back.

### Compound Adjectives and Nouns Are Not Compound Predicates

Remember that a compound predicate contains *two or more simple predicates*. Students sometimes make the mistake of thinking that **compound adjectives** and **nouns** in the complete predicate mean that the predicate is compound. The following sentences *do not* contain compound predicates:

**16**

|  | | SIMPLE PREDICATE | 2 adjectives |
|---|---|---|---|
| 1. | The organic apple | **is** | *pale* and *wormy*. |

|  | | SIMPLE PREDICATE | 3 adjectives |
|---|---|---|---|
| 2. | The new sewer works | **was** | *big, expensive*, and *smelly*. |

| | SIMPLE PREDICATE | 2 adjectives |
|---|---|---|
| 3. You | **had better be** | *safe* than *sorry*. |

|   | SIMPLE PREDICATE | 3 nouns |
|---|---|---|
| 4. He | **was** | a *beggar*, a *thief*, and a *liar*. |
|   | SIMPLE PREDICATE | 2 nouns |
| 5. He | **shot** | a *pheasant* and three *doves*. |

Perhaps the confusion arises in cases like these because the adjectives and nouns in the predicates seem to say something about the subjects. For example, in the sentence *The organic apple is often pale and wormy*, the adjectives do indeed modify the subject.

*pale* and *wormy* organic apple

Nevertheless, they are adjectives and not verbs; therefore, the predicate is not compound. The trick when you are analyzing a predicate is to make certain that you are counting the verbs and not the adjectives and nouns.

## EXERCISE 4

If the sentence has a *SIMPLE* subject or predicate, write *SIMPLE* in the appropriate blank at the left. If the sentence has a *COMPOUND* subject or predicate, write *COMPOUND* in the appropriate blank. (Answers on page 34)

SUBJECT       PREDICATE

_____  _____  1. Trees bent and broke in the storm.

_____  _____  2. Apricots and prunes are dried in the sun.

_____  _____  3. The last game of the season was boring and anti-climactic.

_____  _____  4. John and Paula fight and make-up daily.

_____  _____  5. Rats often grow to be large and mean.

_____  _____  6. Women and money gave him all of his pleasure and caused all of his trouble.

_____  _____  7. The biggest white pine in the country was left uncut.

_____  _____  8. Guam and Tinian are beautiful islands.

_____  _____  9. The sports editor read and reread the article.

_____  _____  10. Jackson first played for Oakland and now plays for New York.

Write one of each kind of sentence as directed.

1. Simple subject and compound predicate

_____

_____

_____

2. Simple subject and simple predicate

_____

_____

_____

3. Compound subject and compound predicate

_____

_____

_____

4. Compound subject and simple predicate

_____

_____

_____

5. A simple sentence with either two adjectives or two nouns placed after the simple predicate

_____

_____

_____

Have your sentences checked.

# LESSON TWO—Some Punctuation Principles

**To Set Off Introductory Words and Phrases**

When should an *introductory word* or *introductory phrase* be punctuated by a comma? Unfortunately, no rule covers every situation, but there are some general guidelines to be followed. An introductory word or phrase needing a comma after it is one that should be followed by a *pause* if it were read aloud. In many cases, your ear will prove a trustworthy guide if you hear the beginning of the sentence. The problem to avoid is reading pauses where they do not occur naturally or where they are not desirable.

## 1. Introductory Transitional Words and Phrases

*Transitional words* and *transitional phrases* are words and groups of words that show the relationship between one statement and another; they make the movement from one sentence to another easier for the reader. The following transitional words and phrases are used to bridge gaps between sentences—to clarify the connection between the thoughts *in separate sentences*. The italicized transitions in the list below are the ones used most frequently; if possible, memorize them.

### Some Introductory Transitional Words and Phrases

| | | |
|---|---|---|
| Accordingly | Granted (If followed by a | Obviously |
| Afterward | pause) | *Of course* |
| Afterwards | Hence | On the whole |
| All in all | Hereafter | Otherwise |
| *Also* (If followed by a | Heretofore | Second |
| pause) | *However* | Similarly |
| As a matter of fact | *In addition* | Still (If followed by a pause) |
| Clearly, then, | In fact | *Then* |
| *Consequently* | In general | To make matters worse |
| Finally (If followed by a | In other words | To be sure |
| pause) | In particular | Thereafter |
| *First* (modern usage) | In short | *Therefore* |
| Firstly (older usage) | In summary | Thereupon |
| *For instance* | Indeed | Third |
| *For example* | Likewise | *Thus* |
| For one thing | *Moreover* | *Unfortunately* |
| Fourth | *Nevertheless* | Worst of all |
| *Furthermore* | Notwithstanding | |

When one of these transitional words or phrases is placed at the very beginning of a sentence, the word or group of words should be separated from the rest of the sentence with *a* **comma** if the separation is to be read as a pause—but avoid putting pauses where they are not needed.

*Examples*

Jerry first wrote some letters. *Afterward* he made several telephone calls. (no pause—no comma)

Jerry first wrote some letters. Afterward , he made several telephone calls. (pause marked by a comma)

**19**

*However* , very few people knew about her sister. (*However* is always followed by a comma)

*Then* the trouble began. (*Then* and other short transitional words are not usually followed by a comma—no pause)

*First* , assemble the shed frame. *Second* , attach the roof pieces. *Third* , screw on the siding panels. (Using commas after these short transitional words creates emphasis on the order in which things are to be done—the commas produce pauses.)

*First* assemble the shed frame. (no comma—less emphasis on *first*)

*Granted* , small cars are economical. *Nevertheless* , they can be dangerous.

*For example* , a box of stale popcorn costs $1.50.

## EXERCISE 6

The *introductory transitional words and phrases* are italicized. Place commas after those that should be followed by a pause marked by a *comma*. (Answers on page 34)

Each time a large ship travels along the East Coast, an ecological disaster is imminent. *For example* _____ a number of accidents on the Atlantic coast have involved huge oil tankers which have collided with other ships, broken in half, or spilled oil during loading or unloading. The damage that occurs with each spill takes place in predictable stages. *First* _____ thousands or even millions of gallons of oil spill into the ocean or harbor. *Then* _____ the winds and currents spread the gooey slick for dozens of miles, fouling the water and shores. *In addition* _____ terrible damage is done to wildlife and marine life, such as ducks and shellfish. The damage done to boats, marinas, docks, and other structures, and the expenses involved in clean-up efforts may cost millions of dollars. *However* _____ the cost of the deaths of thousands of birds and fish is inestimable. *For instance* _____ in the case of one seven-million-gallon spill near Maryland, thousands of birds died within a few hours, and many more died in the weeks that followed due to drastic changes in their shore environment. *Moreover* _____ Chesapeake Bay was declared off limits for shell fishermen for months after because of sludge sinking to the bottom and contaminating the breeding grounds of the clams and mussels. *Unfortunately* _____ more of these disasters are almost certain to occur.

20

## 2. Introductory Words and Phrases That Modify

Other *introductory words and phrases* clarify the ideas within the sentences that they introduce. Some of these sentence openers require commas, and some do not.

*Examples*

>*Tomorrow* Al will begin his new job. (adverb)
>
>*Before noon* it began to rain. (prepositional or adverb phrase)
>
>*Disgusted* , Edna quit the committee. (participle or adjective)
>
>*Although only half finished with his chemistry test* , Fred turned it in anyway. (adverb phrase—see *elliptical clauses*, page 60)
>
>*After the party* , Joe helped Alice clean the kitchen. (prepositional or adverb phrase)
>
>*Vested with unusual powers* , the high priestess was always able to foresee the future. (participle or adjective phrase)

These introductory words and word groups relate to some part of the sentence that follows, usually as modifiers. *When* did it rain? It rained *before noon*. *When* did Joe help Alice? Joe helped Alice *after the party*. Which *high priestess was always able to foresee the future*? The high priestess who was *vested with unusual powers* had that ability. Introductory modifiers always point inward whereas introductory transitional words and phrases always help the reader remember another sentence.

Many *introductory words and phrases that modify* should be set off with commas. A comma separating the introductory part gives it emphasis by creating a pause that keeps the reader from misreading the sentence. In some sentences the need for the comma is obvious.

*MISLEADING*

>*Disgusted* Edna quit the committee.

*CLEAR*

>*Disgusted* , Edna quit the committee.

However, in other sentences the comma after the introductory word or phrase may seem optional—a matter of choice. The modern convention is to read right through most introductory adverbs and short prepositional phrases that act as adverbial modifers, without pausing, *thereby eliminating the need for commas.*

*Examples*

>*There* they found the table they wanted. (adverb)
>
>*Before noon* it began to rain. (prepositional phrase-adverbial)
>
>*Underneath the dashboard* is a fuse panel. (prepositional phrase—adverbial)

**21**

Other *introductory words and phrases* may or may not need commas after them, depending on the sentence and the emphasis desired.

*Examples*

*Later* he was very sorry about his decision. (no pause—adverb)

*Later* **,** her whole world crumbled. (pause—adverb)

*Upon landing* **,** the aliens seized control of New York and Los Angeles. (pause—adverb phrase)

*Just before twelve* **,** three trucks arrived at the store. (pause—adverb phrase—keeps numbers separated)

*Obviously* **,** satisfied customers were more normal than dissatisfied ones. (pause—adverb—prevents *obviously* from being read as an adverb modifying *satisfied*. In this sentence *obviously* functions as an *introductory transitional word.*)

*Obviously* satisfied customers outnumbered the dissatisfied ones. (no pause—adverb-modifying the adjective *satisfied*)

*Wednesday* **,** don't buy bread. (pause—adverb)

### 3. Interjections and Nouns-in-Direct-Address

Introductory *interjections* and *nouns-in-direct-address* are marked by commas although they are neither transitional words nor modifers. (Interjections are seldom used in academic writing.)

**22**     *Examples*

*Good grief* **,** where have you been? (interjection)

*Oh,* what a mess! (interjection)

*Yes,* the answer is correct. (introductory *yes* or *no*)

*Carl,* please mow the lawn now. (noun-in-direct-address)

*Doctor Yarborough,* the insurance form was mailed yesterday. (noun-in-direct-address)

Underline the *introductory word or phrase*. Place a *comma* after it if the comma is needed. If no comma is needed, place a **C** before the sentence. (Check your punctuation with that suggested on page 34.) When your punctuation of any sentence differs from that suggested on the answer page, discuss the sentence with your instructor.

1. After the meeting they stopped for dinner.

2. Prodded by the last acute shortage of natural gas the President has decided to make conservation the basic component of his energy program.

3. To most people conservation of gas means cold homes, bulky sweaters, and wood or coal-burning stoves.

4. However most of the gas consumed in America is used by industry.

5. In the next five years strict conservation methods by industry could reduce its consumption of gas by at least twenty-five percent.

6. For example industrialized nations such as Sweden use only sixty percent of the energy for industry that the United States uses.

7. Before dawn it began snowing.

8. Frustrated George took a break from his math homework.

9. Plagued by machinery breakdowns the company was unable to meet its contracted deadlines for product deliveries.

10. George see if the stove has been turned off.

11. In August the executive council will meet in Seattle.

12. Seeing their chance the three men ran for the woods.

13. Afterwards the meaning of what had happened hit him all at once.

14. Thursday we will meet ten minutes before class.

15. Just beyond the mouth of the bay the glass-bottom boat struck a jagged reef.

## To Separate Adjacent Words and Word Groups

### 1. Coordinate Adjectives

An *adjective* is a word that modifies a noun or pronoun.

*Examples*

Adjective   Noun
Roger negotiated a   **huge**   *settlement*.

Noun   Adjectives
The *castle*, **dark** and **dreary**, stood on the high sea cliff.

**23**

When two or more adjectives are placed before or behind a noun or pronoun, and each adjective modifies the noun or pronoun equally, the adjectives are called *coordinate adjectives*. In other words, each adjective modifies the noun equally but separately, as if the other adjective or adjectives were not there. The easiest way to determine whether adjectives are coordinate is to *reverse their order*; if the adjectives and noun (or pronoun) still make sense together after the order has been switched, the adjectives are coordinate. (Also notice that *and* can be placed between coordinate adjectives.)

*Examples*

| COORDINATE ADJECTIVES | NOT COORDINATE |
|---|---|
| *brisk , bright* day | *raw silk* tie |
| *bright , brisk* day | *silk raw* tie (cannot be reversed) |
| *tall , thin* man | *downtown rush-hour* traffic |
| *thin , tall* man | *rush-hour downtown* traffic (cannot be reversed) |

Place a **comma** between each pair of **coordinate adjectives** unless the adjectives are already separated with a conjunction such as *and, or,* or *but.* After reversing the adjectives and reading the sentence to see if it still makes sense, read the sentence again in the order it is written; the comma separating the coordinate adjectives should mark a pause, or break in speech.

| NO COMMAS | COMMAS NEEDED |
|---|---|
| a *serious municipal court* judge | a *hot , burning* sensation |
| the *suspicious private* detective | a *soiled , ragged* sail |
| a *short nylon* rope | the *tired , hungry deer* hunters |
| a *little black* kitten | a *smelly , moth-eaten wool* sweater |
| a *tiny blue porcelain* dish | an *old , tarnished brass* lamp |
| the *snug* **and** *warm* cabin | the *snug , warm* cabin |
| the cabin, *snug* **and** *warm,* | the cabin , *snug , warm,* |
| the *stern* **but** *fair* captain | the *stern , fair* captain |

## 2. Words and Phrases in a Series

Use a *comma* to separate each *word or phrase* in a *series*, including the conjunction that separates the last two items in the series. (Some instructors consider the comma immediately before this conjunction optional.)

*Examples*

> The flag is *red , white ,* **and** *blue.* (series or *words*)
>
> The crew *checked the tires , filled the gas tank ,* **and** *washed the windshield.*
>
> *Without clearer objectives , better coordination ,* **and** *more adequate funding ,* the new association of district teachers will not be very efficient. (series of *word groups*)

Whenever you wish to emphasize the individual words or word groups making up a series, you can put conjunctions between each of the items. When you do so, **never** separate the items with commas.

*Examples*

> While in the army, we *marched* **and** *marched* **and** *marched.*
> Fred was *big* **and** *mean* **and** *ugly.*
> You should not have *humiliated her* **and** *taken her money.*

**24**

Do **not** place a comma in front of the first word or after the last word in a series.

*Example*

NO    YES       YES

The team was , *tough* , *disciplined* , **and** *enthusiastic*.

YES     YES       NO

They were *tired* , *broke* , **and** *disgusted* , upon arrival in Paris.

Also, do **not** separate consecutive items in a sentence that modify one another, as for example, in a series of prepositional phrases.

*Example*

The bat flew (through the chamber) (between the upper and lower levels) (of the gigantic honeycomb) (of caves).

## EXERCISE 8

Use *commas* to correctly punctuate *adjacent words or word groups* that need them. If a sentence needs no punctuation, write **C** in the left-hand margin next to the sentence. (Answers on page 35)

1. Carol preferred a light moist cake.

2. The little boy was given a big brown puppy for his birthday.

3. He was looking for a small handcarved betel-nut box.

4. The sailboat is thirty-six feet long sloop-rigged and designed for racing.

5. She was shy and frightened and not at all sure she wanted to go through with the interview.

6. With an improved gasoline-mileage rating sleeker body lines and more leg room, the automobile will appeal to more American buyers.

7. The crowd, rowdy belligerent and mean, began to set fires in the bleachers.

8. The cold clear fast-moving stream tumbled down the mountain.

9. The research project involved hundreds of tape-recorded interviews with persons in politics governmental administration and criminal justice.

10. John Foley will formally accept the nomination today or tomorrow.

### To Enclose Words and Phrases That Interrupt Sentences

Often, a word or a phrase that *interrupts* a sentence should *not* be enclosed in commas. Do not use commas if the interrupting word or phrase is absolutely essential in the sentence; do not use commas if the word or phrase is not marked by pauses or special emphasis. By *not* using commas to enclose, you are telling the reader that the word or phrase is an integral part of the sentence and to read it without slowing and without accenting it.

*Examples*

> The boy *defeated* vowed to run for class president again.
>
> The girl *sitting next to me on the bus* needed deodorant.
>
> All of the books *checked out of the library* must be returned by June tenth.
>
> The quiz show *"Twenty Thousand Dollar Pyramid"* was very popular.
>
> She was sure *afterwards* that she had been followed.

Many interrupting words and phrases need to be set apart from the rest of the sentence by commas. However, the following rules are not arbitrary and sometimes overlap. The message behind these suggestions is clear; carefully consider each interrupting word or phrase; then enclose it in commas *if you have a good reason to do so.*

## 1. Transitional Words and Phrases That Interrupt

Any of the same *transitional words and phrases* that are used at the beginning of a sentence may be placed somewhere in the middle of a sentence. See the complete list on page 19.

*Examples*

> , afterwards,
>
> , consequently,
>
> , for example,
>
> , furthermore,
>
> , however,
>
> , in addition,
>
> , nevertheless,
>
> , therefore,

In fact, placing the transitional word or phrase inside a sentence rather than at the beginning may make the transition from a previous sentence more graceful.

*Examples*

> *However,* the lazy summer days seemed to stretch on forever.
>
> The lazy days, *however,* seemed to stretch on forever.

Place a *comma* immediately in front of and immediately after the *interrupting transitional word or phrase,* enclosing it so it will stand out from the rest of the sentence. (The commas should create brief pauses.)

**26**

*Examples*

> Some education experts , *however* , are reluctant to use standardized tests to measure writing competency.
>
> The latest treaty , *for example* , guarantees all airline pilots emergency landing rights.
>
> She was , *afterwards* , shocked at what had happened.

*Many interrupting words or phases need to be set apart from the rest of the sentence by commas . . . .*

## 2. Parenthetical Words and Phrases

Enclose *parenthetical words and phrases* with commas. If the interrupting word or phrase could be placed in parentheses, it normally should be set apart from the rest of the sentence with commas. Placing a word or phrase in commas means that it can be left out without damaging the sentence's meaning.

*Examples*

His performance , *to tell the truth* , was poor.
His performance (to tell the truth) was poor.

John's friend , *a former navy pilot* , wants to hike from Mexico to Canada.
John's friend (a former navy pilot) wants to hike from Mexico to Canada.

The student , *wishing more information* , wrote to the scholarship director.
The student (wishing more information) wrote to the scholarship director.

## 3. To Create Pauses

If you want the reader to *pause* briefly at the beginning and the end of an interrupting word or phrase, enclose the expression with commas. You can test the effects of using or omitting the commas by reading the sentence aloud several times. Your voice will drop slightly when you read the portion of the sentence enclosed in commas.

*Examples*

**27**

PAUSE                    VOICE DROPS                    PAUSE
The primitive tribe      ,      *unknown except to a few anthropolgists*      ,      lived deep in the Amazon rain forest.

                      VOICE
          PAUSE  DROPS  PAUSE
The project         ,      *in general*      ,      is proceeding on schedule.

```
              PAUSE        VOICE DROPS         PAUSE
```
Mary Chavez   ,   *a fourth-year medical student*   ,   planned to set up her practice in Akron, Ohio.

## 4. For Emphasis

Words and phrases are sometimes enclosed in commas for *emphasis*. When commas are used for this purpose, the expression is marked by a pause at the beginning and at the end, but these pauses encourage the reader to accentuate the enclosed word or phrase. Thus, when the sentence is read aloud, the reader will give one or more of the enclosed words a heavier accent than the others. This accent combined with the pauses creates the emphatic tone.

*Examples*

```
              PAUSE    ACCENTED                    PAUSE
```
The president   ,   *the* **ONLY** *person with that authority*   ,   refused to take action.

```
              PAUSE                  ACCENTED    PAUSE
```
The president   ,   *the only person with* **THAT** *authority*   ,   refused to take action.

```
              PAUSE    EMPHASIZED       PAUSE
```
The elephants   ,   *half crazed with fear*   ,   stampeded.

```
          PAUSE              EMPHASIZED              PAUSE
```
George   ,   *thinking that Martians were invading Earth*   ,   began blazing away at the helicopter with his shotgun.

```
          PAUSE   EMPHASIZED   PAUSE
```
And then   ,   *finally*   ,   she found the missing receipt.

## 5. To Prevent Misunderstanding or Awkwardness

At times, interrupting words and phrases must be enclosed in commas to prevent the sentence from being *misread* or sounding *awkward*. These commas help the reader to separate words that might be mistakenly run together with confusing results.

*Examples*

```
      PAUSE            PAUSE
```
Carl   ,   *Frank's brother*   ,   wrote the script. (to *prevent misunderstanding*)

```
              PAUSE                              PAUSE
```
The seasoning   ,   *salt, pepper, garlic, and paprika*   ,   was included in a foil packet. (*to prevent awkwardness*)

**EXERCISE 9**

Enclose the *interrupting words or phrases* in *commas* if the punctuation is needed. If a sentence needs no punctuation, write **C** in the left-hand margin next to the sentence. Study the suggested answers (on page 35); then discuss any that you are not sure about with your instructor.

1. Few people however suspected that Watergate would cause so many problems.
2. The man standing next to me in the bank looked ill.
3. The girl sitting as close to me as possible to keep warm complained about the car's ineffective heater.
4. The new pump for example never has to be lubricated.
5. Her behavior was to my way of thinking admirable.
6. The refugee hoping to gain asylum in America sent a message to the United States Consulate.
7. Joe a former Marine makes the best pizza in town.
8. Alex Haley's book *Roots* has caused millions of Americans to become curious about their ancestors.
9. The show nevertheless will go on.
10. John found out much too late that his application had not been received by the registrar.
11. Mary found out later that a dead mouse was lodged in her heater vent.
12. One of Jim's brothers Tom was an oceanographer at Woods Hole Institute of Oceanography.
13. The head gaskets checked thus far have not been leaking.
14. The solution he was convinced was to start early and get to the best camping spots before the others could claim them.
15. A five-pound roast beef or pork according to personal preference will be awarded free to each customer whose receipt has a star on it.
16. The old law forgotten by most people was now being used to halt new building on farmland around the city.
17. Ben Samuel his football coach agreed to sponsor him in the contest.
18. The main water line corroded through by minerals in the soil will have to be replaced.
19. The audience very amused by the ad lib roared their approval.
20. His homework being finished early a rare event he decided to go see a movie.

## To Separate Words and Phrases at the Ends of Sentences

*Occasionally* a comma is needed to set off a word or phrase at the **end** of a sentence. This comma is used to create an emphatic pause, to prevent misreading, or to keep the sentence from sounding awkward.

### Examples

Drug abuse is on the decline among college students; it is epidemic among the general population , *however.* (transitional word, pause)

He was late to class *as usual.* (no comma—no pause)

He was late to class , *as usual.* (emphatic pause)

Stan hit a grand-slam homerun , *his first.* (emphatic pause)

He rode a motorcycle to the top of Mount Kilamanjaro , *an amazing feat.* (emphatic pause)

The group performed in many small towns all over the country **, *in Michigan, Ohio, Kentucky, Missouri, Montana, and in many other states.* (to prevent misreading)

Then the allied army retreated without warning **, *causing panic and anarchy among the the soldiers and the citizens.* (pause, to prevent misreading)

It was a lively debate **, *to say the least.* (pause, keeps sentence from sounding awkward)

## EXERCISE 10

If the italicized word or phrase *at the end of the sentence* should be set off from the rest of the sentence, punctuate it with a *comma*. If no comma is needed, write **C** in the left-hand margin. Discuss the sentences you do not understand with your instructor. (Answers on page 36)

1. She should apply for the job *nevertheless.*
2. Sam failed his science test *as expected.*
3. She arrived at the airport thirty minutes *before boarding time.*
4. The researcher isolated the virus *a real breakthrough in efforts to find a cure for the disease.*
5. Shirley's doctor said she was suffering from fatigue *caused by months of overwork.*
6. Look in the closet *behind the vacuum cleaner.*
7. The recommendations for water rationing were passed *including the controversial water-meter regulation.*
8. Next time, make sure there is water in the pool *before you dive.*
9. He wanted to hire Sam *Phillip's brother.*
10. He became a King with no power *stripped of his lands and armies.*

**30**

# Unit One Practice Test

This test is just like the *Unit One Posttest* that you must take after completing the work in this unit. If you pass both Part One and Part Two of this practice test, ask your instructor for the *Unit One Posttest*. If you do not pass either the first or second part or both parts, study the test items missed and then restudy the appropriate lesson or lessons before taking the Unit One Posttest. Do not hesitate to ask for assistance. ANSWERS ON PAGE 36. *Your instructor must check items 13-20.*

**Passing Scores**

Part One - 54 points
Part Two 36 points

**Your Scores**

Part One _____ points (60 pts. possible)
Part Two _____ points (40 pts. possible)

**PART ONE: LESSON ONE (3 points each sentence)**

**Directions:**

Place a slash mark (/) between the *complete subject* and the *complete predicate* in each of the following sentences.

1. The small submarine descended rapidly to the sunken freighter.
2. The strange cries were often heard by tenants in the old building.
3. The wino on the corner is actually an undercover police detective.
4. The ecological problems of the proposed project were becoming apparent.

**Directions:**

Identify the *simple subject* and *simple predicate* in each of the following sentences.

| SIMPLE SUBJECT | SIMPLE PREDICATE | |
|---|---|---|
| _____ | _____ | 5. The little red plane with the twin engines is, according to the experts, very fast. |
| _____ | _____ | 6. Why does she have to have this report now? |
| _____ | _____ | 7. Hold this package for me for a few minutes. |
| _____ | _____ | 8. During her last buying trip in England, France, and Germany, she brought back sixty crates of antiques. |

**Directions:**

If the sentence has a simple subject or predicate, write *SIMPLE* in the appropriate blank. If the sentence has a *compound* subject or predicate, write *COMPOUND* in the appropriate blank.

**31**

| SUBJECT | PREDICATE | |
|---|---|---|
| _____ | _____ | 9. The excited soccer fans shoved and pushed one another. |
| _____ | _____ | 10. The lunches in Honolulu were leisurely and filling. |
| _____ | _____ | 11. His teachers and his counselor mean well but do not understand his problem. |
| _____ | _____ | 12. One of the last bobcats in the swamp was shot by a rabbit hunter last winter. |

**Directions:**

Write the kind of *simple sentence* requested.

13. Write a *simple sentence* in which the *subject does something.*

_____

_____

14. Write a *simple sentence* in which *something happens to the subject.*

_____

_____

15. Write a *simple sentence* in which the *complete predicate tells what condition the subject is in.*

_____

_____

16. Write a *simple sentence* in which the *complete predicate tells who or what the subject is.*

_____

_____

**Directions:**

Write one of each kind of *simple* sentence as directed.

17. Simple subject and compound predicate

_____

_____

18. Simple subject and simple predicate

_____

_____

19. Compound subject and compound predicate

_____

**32** _____

20. Compound subject and simple predicate

_____

_____

**PART TWO: LESSON TWO (4 points each sentence)**

**Directions:**

Insert commas where they are needed in the following sentences. If a sentence needs no commas, write *C* in the left-hand margin. The way you punctuate some of the sentences may determine their meaning.

21. Therefore the problem can be solved.
22. Mr. Hardgrass the last farmer in the county with horse-drawn equipment had vowed never to buy a tractor.
23. After the fall he took fewer chances.
24. The new ranch foreman to the old cowboy's astonishment was a woman.
25. Betty was looking for a responsible knowledgeable partner to help her with the buying for her business.
26. Jackie believing nobody refused to see the truth about her lover.
27. Harvey met Jill Lee's cousin at the party.
28. Dreaming of conquest and power the dictator planned to invade the small helpless country of Navarre.
29. The Highway Department will receive bids for the last section of the freeway the link between Sacramento and Stockton.
30. With the wind in her favor that morning Fatima was able to fly the Cessna at a steady 185 miles per hour.

# Answers for Unit One Exercises

**Exercise 1 (page 10)**

1. The subway train / rolled to a stop.
2. He / should have waited for the rain to stop.
3. A stubborn high pressure ridge / kept the winter rains away from the West Coast.
4. The worst time of year for some people / is Christmas.
5. She / bought her boyfriend a gold ring for his birthday.

**Exercise 2 (page 13)**

| | |
|---|---|
| 1. owl | glided |
| 2. boat | was |
| 3. grass | had been piled |
| 4. battery | was |
| 5. movie | will begin |
| 6. place | is |
| 7. [you] | stay |
| 8. Hang-gliding | is |
| 9. one *or* no one | could understand |
| 10. woman | had received |

**Exercise 4 (page 17)**

| | |
|---|---|
| 1. SIMPLE | COMPOUND |
| 2. COMPOUND | SIMPLE |
| 3. SIMPLE | SIMPLE |
| 4. COMPOUND | COMPOUND |
| 5. SIMPLE | SIMPLE |
| 6. COMPOUND | COMPOUND |
| 7. SIMPLE | SIMPLE |
| 8. COMPOUND | SIMPLE |
| 9. SIMPLE | COMPOUND |
| 10. SIMPLE | COMPOUND |

**Exercise 6 (page 20)**

For example,

First,

Then

In addition,

However,

For instance,

Moreover,

Unfortunately,

**Exercise 7 (page 23)**

1. C or *After the meeting* , they stopped for dinner.
2. *Prodded by the last acute shortage of natural gas*, the President has decided to make conservation the basic component of his energy program.
3. C or *To most people* , conservation of gas means cold homes, bulky sweaters, and wood or coal-burning stoves.

4. *However*, most of the gas consumed in America is used by industry.

5. C or *In the next five years* , strict conservation methods by industry could reduce its consumption of gas by at least twenty-five percent.

6. *For example* , industrialized nations such as Sweden only use sixty percent of the energy that the United States uses.

7. C or *Before dawn* , it began snowing.

8. *Frustrated* , George took a break from his math homework.

9. *Plagued by machinery breakdowns* , the company was unable to meet its contracted deadlines for product deliveries.

10. *George* , see if the stove has been turned off.

11. C or *In August* , the executive council will meet in Seattle.

12. *Seeing their chance* , the three men ran for the woods.

13. *Afterwards* , the meaning of what had happened hit him all at once.

14. C or *Thursday* , we will meet ten minutes before class.

15. *Just beyond the mouth of the bay* , the glass-bottom boat struck a jagged reef.

## Exercise 8 (page 25)

1. Carol preferred a light , moist cake.
2. C
3. C
4. The sailboat is thirty-six feet long , sloop-rigged , and designed for racing.

*or*

The sailboat is thirty-six feet long , sloop-rigged and designed for racing.
5. C
6. With an improved gasoline-mileage rating , sleeker body lines , and more leg room, the automobile will appeal to more American buyers.

*or*

With an improved gasoline-mileage rating , sleeker body lines and more leg room , the automobile will appeal to more American buyers.
7. The crowd, rowdy , belligerent , and mean, began to set fires in the bleachers.

*or*

The crowd, rowdy , belligerent and mean, began to set fires in the bleachers.
8. The cold , clear , fast-moving stream tumbled down the mountain.
9. The research project involved hundreds of tape-recorded interviews with persons in politics , governmental administration , and criminal justice.

*or*

The research project involved hundreds of tape-recorded interviews with persons in politics , governmental administration and criminal justice.
10. C

## Exercise 9 (page 29)

1. Few people , however , suspected that Watergate would cause so many problems.
2. C
3. The girl , sitting as close to me as possible to keep warm , complained about the car's ineffective heater.
4. The new pump , for example , never has to be lubricated.
5. Her behavior was , to my way of thinking , admirable.

6. C *or* The refugee , hoping to gain asylum in America , sent a message to the United States Consulate.

7. Joe , a former marine , makes the best pizza in town.

8. C

9. The show , nevertheless , will go on.

10. C *or* John found out , much too late , that his application had not been received by the registrar.

11. C *or* Mary found out , later , that a dead mouse was lodged in her heater vent.

12. One of Jim's brothers , Tom , was an oceanographer at Woods Hole Institute of Oceanography.

13. C

14. The solution , he was convinced , was to start early and get to the best camping spots before the others could claim them.

15. A five-pound roast beef or pork , according to personal preference , will be awarded free to each customer whose receipt has a star on it.

16. The old law , forgotten by most people , was now being used to halt new building on farmland around the city.

17. Ben Samuel , his football coach , agreed to sponsor him in the contest.

18. The main water line , corroded through by minerals in the soil , will have to be replaced.

19. The audience , very amused by the ad lib , roared their approval.

20. His homework being finished early , a rare event , he decided to go see a movie.

**Exercise 10 (page 30)**

1. She should apply for the job , nevertheless.

2. C *or* Sam failed his science test , as expected.

3. C

4. The researcher isolated the virus , a real breakthrough in efforts to find a cure for the disease.

5. C

6. Look in the closet , behind the vaccum cleaner.

7. The recommendations for water rationing were passed , including the controversial water-meter regulation.

8. C *or* Next time , make sure there is water in the pool , before you dive.

9. C *or* He wanted to hire Sam , Phillip's brother.

10. He became a King with no power , stripped of his lands and armies.

**Unit One Practice Test (page 31)**

1. The small submarine / descended rapidly to the sunken freighter.

2. The strange cries / were often heard by tenants in the old building.

3. The wino on the corner / is actually an undercover police detective.

4. The ecological problems of the proposed project / were becoming apparent.

| 5. plane | is |
| 6. she | does have |
| 7. [you] | hold |
| 8. she | brought |
| 9. SIMPLE | COMPOUND |
| 10. SIMPLE | SIMPLE |
| 11. COMPOUND | COMPOUND |
| 12. SIMPLE | SIMPLE |

13.-20. Have your instructor check these sentences.

21. Therefore , the problem can be solved.

22. Mr. Hardgrass , the last farmer in the county with horsedrawn equipment , had vowed never to buy a tractor.

23. C *or* After the fall , he took few chances.

24. The new ranch foreman , to the old cowboy's astonishment , was a woman.

25. Betty was looking for a responsible , knowledgeable partner to help her with the buying for her business.

26. Jackie , believing nobody , refused to see the truth about her lover.

27. C *or* Harvey met Jill , Lee's cousin , at the party.

28. Dreaming of conquest and power , the dictator planned to invade the small , helpless country of Navarre.

29. The Highway Department will receive bids for the last section of the freeway , the link be-between Sacramento and Stockton.

30. With the wind in her favor that morning , Fatima was able to fly the Cessna at a steady 185 miles per hour.

# UNIT TWO

## Writing and Punctuating Compound, Complex, and Compound-Complex Sentences

### Objectives

After completing this unit, you will be able to

1. define the following terms:
   - —phrase
   - —clause
   - —independent clause
   - —dependent clause
   - —conjunction
   - —conjunctive adverb
   - —signal word or phrase
   - —coordination
   - —subordination
   - —compound sentence
   - —complex sentence
   - —compound-complex sentence
2. write and punctuate the following kinds of sentences:
   - —compound
   - —complex
   - —compound-complex
3. define and correct the following kinds of errors:
   - —fragment
   - —run-on
   - —comma-splice

39

# Unit Two Pretest

Before you start to work on the lessons in Unit Two, your instructor may require you to take this pretest to determine which of the three lessons you will need to study. (You may need to study all three.)

You can check many of the items yourself by turning to the ANSWERS ON PAGE 45. *Your instructor must check the following items: 1-2, 4-5, 8-9, 11, 13-14, 17, 19-25.*

| **Passing Scores** | **Your Scores** |
|---|---|
| Part One - 24 points | Part One _____ (28 pts. possible) |
| Part Two - 40 points | Part Two _____ (44 pts. possible) |
| Part Three - 24 points | Part Three _____ (28 pts. possible) |

**PART ONE: LESSON ONE (4 points each)**

1. Define the term *compound sentence*.

_____

_____

2, Write a *compound sentence*, using *and* for a *conjunction*. Punctuate the sentence correctly.

_____

_____

_____

3. (Circle the correct *conjunction*.) After the game they might go to the library, (*and, but, for*) they will probably go to the open house at Shirley's instead.

4. Write a *compound sentence*, using a *semicolon* for a connector. (Do *not* use a conjunctive adverb.)

_____

_____

_____

5. Write a *compound sentence*, using *however* as a *conjunctive adverb*. Punctuate the sentence correctly.

_____

_____

_____

6. (Circle the correct *conjunctive adverb*.) Three experts at stopping undersea oil leaks were rushed to Scotland from Texas; (*for example, however, in addition*), they said it could take more than three weeks to stop the flow of oil into the North Sea.

7. (Circle the letter of the correct answer.) The italicized word in the following sentence is used as
    a. an INTRODUCTORY TRANSITIONAL WORD OR PHRASE
    b. an INTERRUPTING TRANSITIONAL WORD OR PHRASE
    c. a CONJUNCTIVE ADVERB

Winds of up to forty miles an hour whipped up the canyon. *Therefore*, the fire rapidly grew out of control.


## PART TWO: LESSON TWO (4 points each)

8. Define the term *phrase*.

_____

_____


9. Define the term *clause*.

_____

_____


10. (Circle the letter of the correct answer.) The following word groups are
    a. INDEPENDENT CLAUSES
    b. DEPENDENT CLAUSES
    c. PHRASES
    d. SIGNAL WORDS FOR DEPENDENT CLAUSES

    *Dave answered the telephone*
    *the movie began early*
    *go tomorrow*
    *why did they wait so long*

11. Add a *signal word* or *phrase* that will convert the following group of words to a *dependent clause*.

    _____ the major objections of the negotiators were explained to the striking delivery men.

12. Underline each of the *dependent clauses* in the following sentence.

    Before the Spanish began farming and ranching in the valley, the Miwok Indians had several camps where they made baskets and gathered acorns.

13. The sentence below is a *compound* sentence. Convert it to a *complex* sentence by using a *signal word or phrase* to subordinate one of the independent clauses. Punctuate the sentence correctly.

    The alien space ship fired its phaser weapons; the United Federation space ship refused to surrender.

_____

**42** _____

_____

14. Write a *complex sentence* that *begins* with a *dependent clause*.

_____

_____

_____

15. Circle the letter of the sentence that is punctuated correctly.
   a. Before any construction on the dam can begin the seismic safety reports , must be approved.
   b. Before any construction on the dam can begin , the seismic safety reports must be approved.
   c. Before , any construction on the dam can begin , the seismic safety reports must be approved.

16. Which sentence is a *compound-complex* sentence? (Circle the correct letter.)
   a. Although the strawberries were large and red, they were flavorless, and they felt like styrofoam.
   b. After Don saw how much homework was required, he dropped the course and returned his books to the bookstore.
   c. Ann decided to write her outline before the next class meeting so that she could have her teacher check it.

17. Write a *compound-complex* sentence. Punctuate the sentence correctly.

_____

_____

_____

18. (Punctuate the following sentence correctly.) The new pharmacy already has a good business because it is in a professional building with many doctors and business should increase when the nursing home down the block is completed.

## PART THREE: LESSON THREE (4 points each)

19. Define the term *sentence fragment*.

_____

_____

20. Underline the *dependent clause fragment*, and then correct it.
   The young couple did not want children for a few years. Because they both wanted to work. They planned to have two children eventually.

**43**

_____

_____

_____

21. Underline the *phrase fragment* and then correct it.

The FBI arrested three men Wednesday. In connection with the theft of 45,000 pounds of Colombian coffee from a truck parked at a motel.

_____

_____

_____

22. Define the term *run-on sentence.*

_____

_____

23. (Correct the *run-on* error.) An interagency committee found evidence of poor planning and careless accounting procedures their report made ten recommendations for reforming the bureau.

_____

_____

_____

_____

24. Define the term *comma splice.*

_____

_____

25. (Correct the *comma-splice* error.) Man's ancestors, the Homo Habilis, Homo Erectus, and Homo Sapiens, were mainly meat eaters, to hunt animals efficiently, these primitive human-like creatures had to cooperate and share.

_____

_____

_____

_____

**44**

**ANSWERS FOR UNIT TWO PRETEST**

1-2. Instructor checks

3. but

4-5. Instructor checks

6. however

7. a

8-9. Instructor checks

10. a

11. Instructor checks

12. *Before the Spanish began farming and ranching in the valley*, the Miwok Indians had several camps *where they made baskets and gathered acorns.*

13-14. Instructor checks

15. b

16. a

17. Instructor checks

18. The new pharmacy already has a good business because it is in a professional building with many doctors , and business should increase when the nursing home down the block is completed.

19-25. Instructor checks

46

# 2

# LESSON ONE—Compound Sentences

### The Compound Sentence Defined

When two or more closely related simple sentences are connected, the resulting sentence is called a **compound sentence.**

*Example*

The wind blew steadily from the north.

+

The smog cleared

**becomes**

> A **phrase** is a meaningful group of words that does *not* contain a *subject* and a *predicate*.
>
> A **clause** is a meaningful group of words that contains both a *subject* and a *predicate*.

The wind blew steadily from the north, and the smog cleared.

In a compound sentence each of the connected word groups that can stand alone as a simple sentence is an *independent clause.* Each independent clause must have its own subject and predicate.

*Examples*

        INDEPENDENT CLAUSE
            Subject   Predicate
    1. The *wind*      **blew**    steadily from the north

                    **, and**

INDEPENDENT CLAUSE
Subject    Predicate
the  *smog*    **cleared**.


INDEPENDENT CLAUSE
Subject    Predicate
2. The  *school*    **had**    an honor code

, but

INDEPENDENT CLAUSE
Subject    Predicate
*it*    **was** not **working**.


Thus, a compound sentence can be defined as *either*

1. two closely related simple sentences properly connected

**or**

2. two independent clauses of equal importance correctly joined.


### EXERCISE 1

Write *two* definitions of a *compound sentence*. Memorize them. (Answers on page 85)

Definition 1: _____

_____

Definition 2: _____

_____


### Connectors in Compound Sentences—Punctuation

Any of the following *connectors* may be used to join closely related simple sentences (independent clauses) in a compound sentence:

1. *A comma + a conjunction*
2. *A semicolon*
3. *A semicolon + a conjunctive adverb + a comma*

**48**  ### 1. A Comma Plus a Conjunction

A *conjunction* is a *connector word* used to join words and groups of words. The *conjunctions* most commonly used to connect independent clauses (simple sentences) are **and, but**, and **or**. Sometimes the conjunctions **yet** and **for** are used. When a conjunction is used to join independent clauses, a **comma** (,) should be placed in front of the conjunction.

*Examples*

Subject  Predicate  Comma + Conjunction  Subject  Predicate
1. The *teacher*  **was**  late  **, and**  the  *class*  **became**  restless.

Subject  Predicate  Comma + Conjunction  Subject
2. *She*  **ordered**  more French fries  **, but**  the *waiter*  never

Predicate
**brought**  them.

Subject  Predicate  Comma + Conjunction  Subject  Predicate
3. The winter *rains*  **must begin**  soon  **, or**  water *rationing*  **will be**
mandatory next summer.

Subject  Predicate  Comma + Conjunction  Subject
4. *They*  **ordered**  the automobile in February  **, but**  *it*

Predicate
still **had** not **been delivered**  in June.

Subject  Predicate  Comma + Conjunction
5. Many treasure *hunters*  **searched**  for the sunken Spanish galleon  **, for**

Subject  Predicate
*it*  **was loaded**  with gold bars and coins.

## EXERCISE 2

Write *compound sentences*, using the *conjunctions* in the parentheses to connect the independent clauses. Remember to place a *comma* in front of each of the conjunctions. Also, underline each subject *once* and each predicate *twice*.

1. (,and) _____

_____

_____

2. (,but) _____

_____

_____

3. (,or) _____

_____

_____

4. (,yet) _____

_____

**49**

5. (,for) _____

_____

_____

Have your sentences checked.

## Use the Appropriate Conjunctions

When two independent clauses are connected by a comma and a conjunction, one conjunction is usually more appropriate than the others. The conjunction establishes a specific relationship between the two closely related independent clauses it joins; therefore, an improperly used conjunction produces an inaccurate or awkward sentence. Always choose the conjunction that will state the close connection between the two independent clauses most exactly.

*Examples*

1. The automobile flipped over**, and** the driver was thrown out onto the busy street.

    The conjunction *and* is used to explain that *in addition* to what happened in the first independent clause, the event described in the second independent clause also occurred.

2. The driver was not hurt badly**, but** he was scraped and bruised.

    *But* shows a contrast between what is said in the first independent clause and what is said in the second independent clause. *But* can also be used to show opposition: "The witnesses called the driver reckless, **but** the driver denied that he was."

3. The driver skidded across the busy right-hand lane like a rag doll**, yet** two cars, a bus, and a cement truck managed to miss him.

    *Yet* like *but* is used to show contrast or opposition. However, *yet* has been used in this sentence to imply that what happened in the second independent clause was not what most readers would have expected to have happened after reading the first independent clause.

4. He will ride to the hospital for a checkup**, or** he will see his own doctor tomorrow.

    *Or* connects the two independent clauses that describe *alternate* possibilities.

5. The wrecker towed the man's automobile away**, for** the wrecked vehicle could no longer be driven.

    *For* should be used as a conjunction when a connector that means *because* is needed. The conjunction *for* should not be confused with the preposition *for*, as in the sentence, "He began to look *for* a new car."

Be particularly careful to avoid the careless use of the conjunction *and* in sentences whose meaning could be made clearer by substituting *but, yet*, or *or*.

**50**

| *Careless* | *Clearer* |
|---|---|
| Monday morning at the office was calm*, **and*** the rest of the week was chaotic. | Monday morning at the office was calm*, **but*** the rest of the week was chaotic. |
| She can cope with the strange habits of her husband*, **and*** she can ask for a divorce and look for a "normal" man with whom to live. | She can cope with the strange habits of her husband, ***or*** she can ask for a divorce and look for a "normal" man with whom to live. |

Choose the conjunction that most accurately relates the second independent clause to the first independent clause. (Answers on page 85)

1. The automobiles collided head-on at sixty-five miles an hour, (*and, but, yet*) no one was killed.
2. After the dance they might stop for a pizza, (*and, but, yet*) they might order hamburgers and milkshakes instead.
3. The Coast Guard report blamed the captain of the tanker for running aground, (*and, but, or*) the captain claimed his navigation instruments were faulty.
4. Someone should tell him to come to class more regularly, (*and, for, or*) he will fail the course.
5. Joan has beautiful hair and eyes, (*and, but, or*) her appearance is spoiled by her poor posture.
6. The sea was calm, (*and, but, yet*) the sky was blue and cloudless.
7. He purchased the antique Korean chest, (*and, but, for*) he thought it was a good investment.
8. Harold rehearsed for the interview for days, (*and, but, yet*) he was nervous as the Personnel Director began to ask questions.
9. She will look for a job, (*and, but, or*) she will go to school instead.
10. We cannot come to dinner next Saturday, (*and, but, yet*) we can come the Saturday after.

## 2. The Semicolon

Another commonly used technique for combining closely related independent clauses (simple sentences) is the *semicolon* (;). A better name for the semicolon might be "semiperiod" since the period can be used anywhere a semicolon can be used.

*Example*

> Walking is good for your health.
> You should do more of it.

**becomes**

> Walking is good for your health; you should do more of it.

The advantage gained by using a semicolon is that the reader will move more rapidly through what you have written. The semicolon tells the reader to take a briefer pause at the juncture of the two independent clauses than if a period had been used to separate the two clauses. The semicolon also emphasizes the close relationship between two inde-

51

pendent clauses in a compound sentence more than a conjunction used with a comma. The occasional use of a semicolon marks the style of a knowledgeable writer, but the semicolon should not be overused.

*Examples*

George and the others made the fateful decision on Tuesday. *They could wait no longer; they knew it.* The snow had been falling on the mountain all night, and by noon the wreckage of the plane would be completely covered. *John had to hike down the mountain for help; no one would see them from the air.*

**EXERCISE 4**

Write *two* definitions of a *compound sentence.* If you have forgotten the definitions since the last time you wrote them, memorize them again. (Answers on page 85)

Definition 1: _____

_____

Definition 2: _____

_____

**EXERCISE 5**

Write *five* compound sentences, using *semicolons* as connectors between the independent clauses. Label the subject and predicate in each independent clause.

1. _____

_____

_____

2. _____

_____

_____

3. _____

**52** _____

_____

4. _____

_____

5.

Have the sentences checked.

### 3. A Semicolon Plus a Conjunctive Adverb

A *semicolon* and a *conjunctive adverb* can be used together very effectively to join two independent clauses in a compound sentence. The word *conjunct* means "cojoined," or "bound in close association"; a *conjunctive* is a connective used to "link" or "join." Thus, *conjunctive adverbs* are adverbs and short adverb phrases used not as modifiers but as connectors to join closely related independent clauses.

*Example*

The students were given only fifteen minutes to complete the fifty-question test*;* ***consequently***, many students were unable to finish it.

#### Some Conjunctive Adverbs*

| | | |
|---|---|---|
| ;accordingly, | ;hence, | ;obviously, |
| ;afterward, | ;hereafter, | ;*of course,* |
| ;afterwards, | ;heretofore, | ;on the whole, |
| ;all in all, | ;*however*, | ;otherwise, |
| ;*also*, | ;*in addition*, | ;second, |
| ;as a matter of fact, | ;in fact, | ;similarly, |
| ;clearly, then, | ;in general, | ;still, |
| ;*consequently*, | ;in other words, | ;*then*(,) |
| ;finally, | ;in particular, | ;thereafter, |
| ;*first*, | ;in short, | ;*therefore*, |
| ;*for instance*, | ;in summary, | ;thereupon, |
| ;*for example*, | ;indeed, | ;third, |
| ;for one thing, | ;likewise, | ;*thus*, |
| ;fourth, | ;*moreover*, | ;to be sure, |
| ;*furthermore*, | ;*nevertheless*, | ;to make matters worse, |
| ;granted, | ;notwithstanding, | ;unfortunately, |
| | | ;worst of all, |

*The most frequently used conjunctive adverbs are italicized.

A *semicolon* is always placed in front of a conjunctive adverb used as a connective between two independent clauses.

*Example*

World weather patterns probably will undergo radical shifts in the near future*; therefore,* agricultural expansion is not recommended.

Moreover, except when using *then*, a comma ordinarily should be placed immediately after a conjunctive adverb connecting two independent clauses. Do not follow *then* with

**53**

a comma when using it as a conjunctive adverb. (If no pause is desired after *then*, *thus*, and other *short* conjunctive adverbs, use *no* comma.)

*Example*

Food production in the world today is sufficient to eliminate starvation; *however,* a more effective distribution system must be developed during the next ten years. By 1988 a centralized computer system will balance world supply and demand information for agricultural commodities; *then* enormous sailing ships will transport the products across the seas to special distribution centers.

## EXERCISE 6

Define a *compound sentence two* different ways. (Answers on page 85)

Definition 1: _____

_____

Definition 2: _____

_____

## EXERCISE 7

Write *compound sentences*, using the following *conjunctive adverbs*. Punctuate the sentences correctly.

1. (also) _____

_____

_____

2. (consequently) _____

_____

_____

3. (for example) _____

**54**

_____

4. (furthermore) _____

_____

_____

5. (however) _____

_____

_____

6. (moreover) _____

_____

_____

7. (nevertheless) _____

_____

_____

8. (of course) _____

_____

_____

9. (then) _____

_____

_____

10. (therefore) _____

_____

_____

Have your work checked.

## Choosing the Appropriate Conjunctive Adverb

Properly used, the *conjunctive adverb* adds more emphasis than the ordinary conjunction, such as *and* or *but*. Although there may be more than one correct conjunctive adverb for combining closely related simple sentences, there is usually one that is preferable over the others because it makes the logical connection between the two independent clauses the clearest. And, conversely, not just any conjunctive adverb will do, for the wrong connective word will confuse the logical relationship between the independent clauses being joined. The following table illustrates the proper function for the most commonly used conjunctive adverbs:

**55**

| *Relationship To Be Established* | Conjunctive Adverb To Use |
|---|---|
| addition, comparison | *moreover, furthermore, in addition* |
| contrast, difference, opposition | *however, nevertheless* |

| as a result, conclusion | *therefore, thus, consequently* |
| concession | *of course* |
| emphasis | *indeed, unfortunately* |
| illustration | *for instance, for example* |

## EXERCISE 8

Use appropriate *conjunctive adverbs* to join the following independent clauses. Remember to punctuate each compound sentence correctly. (Answers on page 85)

1. The road between Pollock Pines and Omo Ranch was quite rough _____ we found it more comfortable to drive slower than usual.

2. In the spring the tiny streams become roaring rivers _____ in the summer the rivers dry up into little rivulets.

3. Their boat became becalmed near Martha's Vineyard _____ they spent the night waiting for the wind to return.

4. Kent seldom bothers to attend class or read his assignments _____ he has never even taken his first test.

5. "Heart of Darkness" is undoubtedly one of Conrad's best short stories _____ "The Secret Sharer" is also one of his better stories.

6. People are reading less fiction this year _____ non-fiction has become much more popular than it was last year.

7. More students are enrolling in college _____ they are taking fewer courses each semester than in the past.

8. The commentator named the five great threats to humanity _____ none of the listeners seemed to care.

9. She is teaching some unusual home economics courses _____ one of them is called "Brown Bag Gourmet."

10. His stocks plummeted in value _____ he sold them immediately.

### Avoid Confusion

The words and phrases listed in this lesson as *conjunctive adverbs* also are listed in Unit One, where they are called either *introductory transitional words and phrases* (see pages 19-26) or *interrupting transitional words and phrases* (see pages 19-26). These same words and phrases can be used in *three different positions* for *three different purposes.* You must understand each of the purposes and the punctuation that must be used when one of these words or phrases is used in a particular position.

**56**

1. AT THE BEGINNING OF A SENTENCE as an *Introductory Transitional Word or Phrase*

   *Example*

   Many of the students had part-time jobs in the afternoon. *Consequently*, they refused to enroll in classes after twelve o'clock.

2. IN THE MIDDLE OF A SENTENCE as an *Interrupting Transitional Word or Phrase*

   *Example*

   Many of the students had part-time jobs. They refused , *consequently*, to enroll in any classes after twelve o'clock.

3. TO CONNECT TWO SENTENCES (TWO INDEPENDENT CLAUSES) as a *Conjunctive Adverb*

   *Example*

   Many of the students had part-time jobs ; *consequently* , they refused to enroll in any classes after twelve o'clock.


**EXERCISE 9**

In the blank at the left, write the letter that correctly identifies the type of word or phrase that is italicized. Then insert in the sentence the punctuation that should accompany the word or phrase. (Answers on page 85)

   A. *INTRODUCTORY TRANSITIONAL WORD OR PHRASE*
   B. *INTERRUPTING TRANSITIONAL WORD OR PHRASE*
   C. *CONJUNCTIVE ADVERB*

_____ 1. People make a mistake when they assume creativity deals only with writing, art, and music. *For example* a businessman can be as creative as a painter.

_____ 2. *Moreover* a creative person does not have to be suffering or unstable.

_____ 3. After a good night's sleep most people are energetic and efficient *however* after a poor night's sleep people are usually slow and ineffective.

_____ 4. George was *to be sure* an old-fashioned boss who believed in treating his son like a regular employee. The son *however* wanted to "step into his father's shoes" immediately.

_____ 5. The company was so bound up in rules, regulations, and other red tape that the executives did not really lead the employees *in fact* a real leader would have been feared and resented.


# LESSON TWO—Complex Sentences

### The Complex Sentence Defined

A *complex sentence* is a sentence that includes one *independent clause* and one or more *dependent clauses*.

*Examples*

| INDEPENDENT CLAUSE | DEPENDENT CLAUSE |
|---|---|
| 1. They wanted to buy the restaurant | *although they had no restaurant management experience.* |

57

2. *As the men rowed across the inlet,*     he saw the fortress

DEPENDENT CLAUSE
*that was to become his prison.*

## Independent and Dependent Clauses

An *independent clause* is a group of words that can stand alone as a simple sentence; each independent clause has its own subject and predicate.

*Example*

         Subject  Predicate

The   *storm*  **dumped**    eight inches of snow on Chicago.

A *dependent clause* is also a meaningful group of words that contains a subject and a predicate, but it *cannot* stand alone as a simple sentence. A dependent clause must always be connected to an independent clause; a dependent clause is only *a part of a sentence.* A dependent clause includes *three* main elements:

1. A signal word or phrase
2. A subject
3. A predicate

*Examples*

DEPENDENT CLAUSE

Signal Word      Subject  Predicate
1. **Before**     the *terrorists* **could grab** their weapons,  the commandoes burst into the airport lounge.

DEPENDENT CLAUSE

    Signal Word & Subject     Predicate
2. The terrorists, ***who* were** completely **surprised**,  fought back furiously.

DEPENDENT CLAUSE

    Signal Word   Subject  Predicate
3. Three of the hostages were found dead  **after** the *shooting*  **stopped.**

## Signal Words and Signal Phrases

The following words and phrases often signal the beginning of a dependent clause:

| | | |
|---|---|---|
| after | if | until |
| although | if ever | what |
| as | if only | whatever |
| as close as | lest | what if |
| as if | like | whatsoever |
| as long as | now | when |
| as often as | now that | whenever |
| as soon as | once | where |
| as though | provided | whereas |

| | | |
|---|---|---|
| because | so far as | whether |
| before | so long as | whether . . . or |
| but that | so much as | which |
| but what | so near as | whichever |
| except | so that | while |
| except that | such that | who |
| how | than | whoever |
| in case | that | whom |
| in order that | though | whomever |
| in which | till | whose |
| provided that | unless | whosoever |
| since | wherever | why |

Upon encountering one of the *signal words or signal phrases*, check further to see if the signal word or phrase is followed by a subject and a predicate. If it is, the group of words is a dependent clause. (If the signal word or phrase is not followed by a subject and a predicate, the dependent word group is a *phrase*.) Remember, a dependent clause is like an independent clause in that both have a subject and verb; however, the dependent clause, unlike the independent clause, cannot be a sentence by itself.

*Examples*

Independent Clause    *We walked down the aisle.*

Dependent Clause      *After we walked down the aisle*

The first example is a complete sentence. The sentence has a subject and a predicate, and it makes sense by itself. However, the very same clause becomes a dependent clause when the signal word *after* is placed before the independent clause. The resulting dependent clause is no longer a sentence; it must be joined with an independent clause. When a *relative pronoun*, for example, *that, what, which, who* and *whom*, is used as a signal word, it often does double duty: it functions as the signal word and as the subject of the dependent clause.

*Examples*

Signal Word & Subject    Predicate
The sailors    *who*    **ate** and **drank** too much became sick.


Signal Word & Subject    Predicate
The automobile    *that*    **burns** too much gasoline may soon be unpopular.

*. . . independent and dependent clauses . . .*

**59**

INCOMPLETE DEPENDENT CLAUSES (ELLIPTICAL CLAUSES)

Some dependent clauses look like phrases because they are incomplete. In an *incomplete dependent clause*— also called an **elliptical clause**—part of the clause has been omitted even though it is in the writer's mind. The same punctuation rules that apply to complete dependent clauses apply to *elliptical* dependent clauses as well.

*Examples*

INCOMPLETE

*While eating,*   he read a magazine.

COMPLETE

*While (he was) eating,*   he read a magazine.

INCOMPLETE

That room is larger   *than the other.*

COMPLETE

That room is larger   *than the other one (is large).*

**EXERCISE 10**

Define each of the following terms. Write an example of each term.

PHRASE

_____

_____

Example

_____

CLAUSE

_____

_____

**60**   Example _____

_____

INDEPENDENT CLAUSE

_____

Example _____

_____

## SIGNAL WORD OR PHRASE

_____

_____

Example of Signal Word _____

Example of Signal Phrase _____

## DEPENDENT CLAUSE

_____

_____

Example _____

_____

## INCOMPLETE (ELLIPTICAL) DEPENDENT CLAUSE

_____

_____

Example _____

_____

## SIMPLE SENTENCE

_____

_____

Example _____

_____

## COMPOUND SENTENCE

_____

_____

Example _____

_____

COMPLEX SENTENCE

_____

_____

Example _____

_____

_____

Have your definitions and examples checked.

**EXERCISE 11**

In the blank at the left identify the word or word group by writing one of the following labels: INDEPENDENT CLAUSE, DEPENDENT CLAUSE, PHRASE, SIGNAL WORD, SIGNAL PHRASE. (Answers on page 86)

_____  1. in the third room

_____  2. after the rain began

_____  3. so that

_____  4. the movie was seen by millions of viewers

_____  5. which the list included

_____  6. driving carefully

_____  7. whenever it snowed

_____  8. the reorganization was complete

_____  9. if

_____  10. while driving carefully

_____  11. we went to the hockey game

_____  12. a boat on the bay

_____  13. provided that

_____  14. on a bench under the tall elm

_____  15. although

_____  16. who stood beside him through the crisis

_____  17. feeling dizzy

_____  18. kings and queens lived and died in the castle's great halls

_____  19. while studying her French

_____  20. than

62

Add a *signal word* or *signal phrase* that will convert the independent clause to a dependent clause. Underline the simple subject *once* and the simple predicate *twice*.

1. _____ the earthquake rattled the whole building

2. _____ they painted the living room

3. _____ six hundred students attended the concert

4. _____ she wanted (use a relative pronoun)

5. _____ flying to Phoenix (make an elliptical dependent clause)

Have the clauses checked.

## Subordination

In the last lesson you learned how to *compound* ideas in *compound sentences*; you learned to connnect two or more independent clauses with a connector. Each independent clause expressed an idea approximately *equal* in importance to the other independent clause with which it was connected. The clauses were *coordinated*.

*Example*

John loved Mary, but Mary loved Joe.

But a *complex sentence* contains one independent clause and at least one dependent clause, and each dependent clause expresses an idea that is not as important as the idea in the independent clause. The *main idea* of the sentence is communicated in the independent clause, and lesser ideas are *subordinated* in dependent clauses. Dependent clauses cannot stand alone as sentences; they act as modifiers, making the meaning of the main idea clearer.

*Examples*

INDEPENDENT CLAUSE
1. The glider soared up and away from the cliff
DEPENDENT CLAUSE

| Signal Phrase | Subject | Predicate | |
|---|---|---|---|
| **as soon as** | *it* | **hit** | the updraft. |

The *main idea* in the above sentence is that the glider soared up and away from the cliff; this idea is stated in the independent clause. The *subordinate idea* is expressed in the dependent clause. Although not as important as the main idea, the subordinate idea does add a detail; the dependent clause tells WHEN the glider was able to sail beyond the cliff.

**63**

INDEPENDENT CLAUSE
2. Sue wanted to fly the huge orange sail kite
DEPENDENT CLAUSE

| Signal Word | Subject | Predicate |
|---|---|---|
| **that** | her *brother* | **had built**. |

The main idea is that Sue wanted to fly the orange sail kite. The fact that her brother built it is not as important as the main idea; the dependent clause modifies the independent clause by telling *which* kite Sue wanted to fly—the one built by her brother.

**EXERCISE 13**

Underline all *dependent clauses* in the following sentences. Some sentences contain more than one dependent clause. (Answers on page 86)

1. Although his friends are all corrupt, he insists that his hands are clean.

2. He was not afraid of the growling dog because he had his lucky coin in his pocket.

3. Mayor Jones, whom everyone considered a liar, stated that he would not seek another term.

4. Since he celebrated his fortieth birthday, he had begun to spend more time with his family.

5. The dress was the one that she had been hoping to find on sale.

**EXERCISE 14**

1. *Explain* how ideas are **coordinated** in a *compound sentence*.

_____

_____

_____

2. *Show* how ideas are **coordinated** in a *compound sentence* by writing an example.

_____

_____

_____

3. *Explain* how an idea is **subordinated** in a *complex sentence*.

_____

_____

_____

**64**

4. Write an *example* to demonstrate how an idea can be **subordinated** in a *complex sentence*.

_____

_____

_____

Convert each *compound sentence* to a *complex sentence* by using a *signal word or signal phrase* to *subordinate* one of the independent clauses. Underline the signal word or phrase that you have put in the place of the conjunction or semicolon.

1. The patrol boat fired its cannon at the surfaced submarine, and the submarine fired three torpedoes at the patrol boat.

   _____

   _____

   _____

2. Ann was not prepared for Freshman Composition; she enrolled in a remedial English class.

   _____

   _____

   _____

3. The oil executive already has tremendous political power, and he does not need to run for political office.

   _____

   _____

   _____

4. The tanker split in half, and seven million gallons of oil poured into the surf.

   _____

   _____

   _____

5. He does not exercise regularly, but he eats moderately.

   _____

   _____

Have your sentences checked.

## Dependent Clauses Are Used to Introduce, to Interrupt, and to Conclude

The *dependent clause* in a complex sentence may appear at the *beginning*, in the *middle*, or at the *end* of the sentence.

### Examples

1. *Although the dog looked like a mongrel*, it was actually very rare and expensive.
2. The dog, *although it looked like a mongrel*, was actually very rare and expensive.
3. The dog was actually very rare and expensive *although it looked like a mongrel*.

### When To Use Commas In Complex Sentences

When a dependent clause *introduces* a sentence—when the dependent clause is placed at the *beginning* of a sentence—place a comma at the end of the dependent clause to separate it from the independent clause that follows it.

### Examples

*When Beth typed her term paper,* she forgot to include her footnotes.

*After jogging,* Sue always takes a shower and a nap. (*elliptical clause*)

If a dependent clause that *interrupts* the independent clause in a complex sentence is *essential* to the sentence, *do not* surround it with commas. But if the interrupting dependent clause *is not needed, enclose* it with a pair of commas. In other words, if the sentence makes sense when it is read without the dependent clause—if the sentence still says what you want it to say after the dependent clause is omitted—set it off with commas. On the other hand, if the meaning of the sentence is changed or if it is not clear after the dependent clause is removed, do not set off the dependent clause by placing a comma immediately before it and one immediately after it.

### Examples

| | |
|---|---|
| *non-essential* | Sheri, *whom we saw last night,* works in the library. |
| *essential* | The girl *whom we saw last night* works in the library. |
| *non-essential* | Dessert, *which John likes best,* will be served later. |
| *essential* | The part of the dinner *that John likes best* is dessert. |
| *non-essential* | Inflation, *which was also a problem in ancient Rome,* will continue during the next decade. |
| *essential* | The inflation *that reduced this company's investment fund this year* can be expected to continue next year. |
| *non-essential* | John worked as a real estate salesman, *before marrying Jody,* selling mostly commercial property. (*elliptical clause*) |
| *essential* | The solar energy panels *when properly placed* provide enough heat to warm the swimming pool. (*elliptical clause*) |

**66**

An interrupting dependent clause that follows a name is customarily considered to be *non-essential,* even if the person reading the sentence does not know the person named.

Mrs. Smith, *who is one of the Budget Committee members,* will be appointed to the Steering Committee.

Whenever possible, refrain from using a comma to separate an independent clause and a dependent clause that follows it at the end of a sentence. You must have a very good reason for using a comma to set off a dependent clause at the end of a sentence. Usually no comma is needed.

*Examples*

He will attend the university *if he is accepted as a transfer student.*
She worked on her paper *until she had to leave for work.*
They knew *that the situation was hopeless.*
Is she more color blind *than you?* (elliptical clause)

Nevertheless, a comma placed between an independent clause and the dependent clause that follows at the end of a sentence is sometimes helpful to the reader. A comma may be used when an emphatic pause between the independent clause is desired or when the dependent clause states clearly extra, added information not absolutely needed in the sentence.

*Examples*

He insisted on pursuing his reckless course of action, *even though he had been warned against such actions many times.* (emphatic pause)
The news angered the old soldier, *as most news usually did.* (dependent clause not needed)
He will attend the university, *if he is accepted as a transfer student.* (emphatic pause)
Bob wrote the term paper, *although poorly.* (elliptical clause, emphatic pause)

A comma should be used to separate an independent clause from a dependent clause following it when the comma will make the meaning of the sentence clearer or prevent the sentence from sounding awkward.

*Examples*

The narrative account of Chief Joseph's defeat portrayed the chief as being very noble and very wise, *which according to all historical accounts he was.*
She understood that theory, *that each student has a learning style.*

**EXERCISE 16**

Write *complex sentences* according to the following directions.

1. Write a complex sentence *beginning* with a dependent clause. Punctuate it correctly.

2. Write a complex sentence with a dependent clause that *interrupts* the independent clause. In this sentence make the interrupting dependent clause *essential* and punctuate it correctly.

_____

_____

_____

3. Write another complex sentence with an interrupting dependent clause. In this sentence make the interrupting dependent clause *non-essential* and punctuate it accordingly.

_____

_____

_____

4. Write a complex sentence in which the independent clause is *followed* by a dependent clause without an emphatic pause.

_____

_____

_____

5. Write another complex sentence that *ends* with a dependent clause. Create an emphatic pause between the independent and dependent clauses.

_____

_____

_____

6. Write a complex sentence that contains an *elliptical clause*—at the beginning, in the middle, or at the end. Punctuate the sentence correctly.

_____

_____

_____

Have your sentences checked.

**EXERCISE 17**

*Punctuate* the following complex sentences correctly. Some sentences will need no commas. Some sentences contain an *elliptical clause* in addition to a regular dependent clause. (Answers on page 86)

1. Although the weather forecast predicted rain the sky was clear and blue.
2. The sky was dark and threatening although the weather forecast called for clear skies.

3. The parking lot was always full when classes started in the fall.
4. When the semester was almost over there were many empty parking spaces.
5. The pants that she purchased Saturday were marked down for a sale on Monday.
6. The blazer which she thought about during her coffee break was not marked down.
7. Ralph knew that he had made a mistake that he had made a terrible mistake.
8. As far as they could tell after consulting several experts no tidal wave would follow the small quake.
9. As predicted Arnold Fletcher who had conducted the civic orchestra for ten years wanted to retire at the end of the spring concert series.
10. The settler who built the cabin never did farm the land after clearing it.

## Compound-Complex Sentences

A *compound-complex sentence* is a sentence that contains at least *two* independent clauses and one or more dependent clauses.

*Examples*

INDEPENDENT CLAUSE #1
1. The Air Force interceptors streaked into the sky, //
INDEPENDENT CLAUSE #2
and the ground crew watched the formation //
DEPENDENT CLAUSE
*until it was out of sight.*

INDEPENDENT         Dependent Clause #1
2. The radar operators, // *who were keeping track of heavy traffic,* //
CLAUSE #1      Dependent Clause #2
tracked it // *until it entered another control section*; //
INDEPENDENT CLAUSE #2
then they turned their attention to other aircraft.

## EXERCISE 18

Write three *compound-complex* sentences.

1. _____

_____

_____

2. _____

**69**

_____

_____

3. _____

   _____

   _____

Have the sentences checked.

**EXERCISE 19**

Punctuate the following sentences correctly. *Simple, compound, complex,* and *compound-complex* sentences are included. A few sentences need no commas. (Answers on page 87)

1. When we got home her father was waiting at the front door.
2. While the snow was falling no traffic moved.
3. We rode snowmobiles during the morning and went skiing in the afternoon.
4. Jan and Ricky when they were much younger were always in trouble.
5. She kept entering million-dollar contests but she never won.
6. We will leave whenever you are ready.
7. The girl with sad eyes looks very lonely.
8. When our group was asked for our report we could only laugh.
9. Although it was fall everyone in class seemed to have spring fever.
10. Geometry which is not my favorite subject is the only class I hate to attend.
11. The lady who lives behind my house grows beautiful roses.
12. Avery Anderson who delivers our mail is getting married next Saturday.
13. However the automobile was not for sale.
14. The frightened horse moreover stepped on the fallen rider.
15. Furthermore the yelling grooms made the horse more excited and he ran into the side of the judge's car.
16. Jaguars which I like better than Corvettes are fine sport cars.
17. Joe is prejudiced against women he thinks they are incapable of being anything but mothers.
18. While we were in Ireland last year it rained and rained and rained.
19. American River canoe trips produce sore muscles sunburned skin and many happy memories.
20. We knew of course that exploring the caves was dangerous nevertheless we entered the cave without food rope or flashlights.
21. They could have taken the ferry across to Victoria but chose not to visit the city.
22. Chuck a guy we met at the bottom of the canyon and a few other people were about ten minutes behind us.
23. We had been told that snakes come out for warmth at night.
24. When Jane and I hiked closer to the falls the noise became so loud that we had to scream to hear one another although we were only ten feet apart.
25. Pro-abortion arguments have been based on the premise that pregnant women should have the final say that men have too long made these decisions from their own perspective for men are not the ones who must actually bear the babies.

# LESSON THREE—Three Constructions to Avoid: Sentence Fragments, Run-on Sentences, and Comma Splices

### Sentence Fragments

A *sentence fragment* is a part of a sentence punctuated as if it were a complete sentence. Although sentence fragments are sometimes used effectively by professional writers, especially novelists and journalists, sentence fragments are usually considered to be inappropriate in academic writing. Any sentence fragment in one of your compositions —EVEN IF YOU HAVE INCLUDED IT PURPOSELY—may make your reader think that you do not understand correct sentence structure. In general, sentence fragments should be avoided; they will be marked as errors in any writing you do for the assignments in this book.

### Dependent Clause Fragments

The sentence fragment most commonly discovered in students' compositions is the *dependent clause* that has been left to stand alone.

*Examples*

When we returned at two in the morning.
Which was the kind they wanted.
Who always criticized the manager's policies.
Where the boys are.

71

Each of the dependent clauses above is a sentence fragment because it has been placed alone, capitalized at the beginning, and punctuated with a period at the end. However, each sentence fragment above can be corrected easily either by attaching it to an independent clause or by incorporating it in an independent clause. Attach the sentence fragment to the sentence in front of it—if the two belong together—or join the fragment to the sentence that follows if the two parts fit together smoothly. In some cases, however, merely joining the fragment to the sentence that precedes or follows it will not work. In these cases, develop the sentence fragment into a complete sentence that can stand by itself.

*Examples*

| WRONG | CORRECTED |
|---|---|
| We stayed out much later than we had planned. *When we returned home at two in the morning.* We were surprised to see the lights on. | We stayed out much later than we had planned. *When we returned home at two in the morning,* we were surprised to see the lights on. |

The dependent clause has been attached to the sentence that follows it because the two parts fit together smoothly to form one *complex sentence*. The dependent clause would not fit well with the sentence before it.

| WRONG | CORRECTED |
|---|---|
| They purchased a nineteenth-century Korean chest made of persimmon wood. *Which was the kind of chest they wanted.* They placed it in the living room. | They purchased a nineteenth-century Korean chest made of persimmon wood, *which was the kind of chest they wanted.* They placed it in the living room. |

In this example the sentence fragment error has been corrected by joining the dependent clause to the sentence in front of it, making a *complex sentence*. The dependent clause cannot logically be connected to the sentence that follows it.

| WRONG | CORRECTED |
|---|---|
| Adams was suddenly praising the manager's work. *Who had always criticized the manager's policies.* | Adams, *who had always criticized the manager's policies*, was suddenly praising the manager's work. |

The dependent clause by itself is an illogical fragment that makes the sentence before it unclear. The sentence fragment has been corrected by incorporating the dependent clause in the complete sentence. The meaning of the resulting complex sentence is clear.

| WRONG | CORRECTED |
|---|---|
| Sue is crazy about boys all of a sudden. Everyone knows where to look for her. *Where the boys are.* | Sue is crazy about boys all of a sudden. Everyone knows where to find her. She can be found *where the boys are.* |

The sentence fragment in the above example has been corrected by developing the dependent clause into a *complex sentence*.

This particular dependent clause can also be attached to the sentence in front of it, provided that the resulting complex sentence is punctuated correctly.

**72**

Everyone knows where to find her: *where the boys are.* (*colon* used)

or

Everyone knows where to find her—*where the boys are.* (*dash* used)

First, underline the *dependent clause fragment*; then correct it either by connecting it to the sentence before or after it, or by developing the fragment in a sentence. Punctuate each sentence correctly.

1. The young couple were unable to buy an automobile when they got married. Although they did not seem to mind. They wanted to save enough money to buy a house.

_____

_____

_____

2. When the game was over, we all stopped for pizza on the way home. Because we did not have to get up early the next day. We were in no hurry to leave the restaurant.

_____

_____

_____

3. Although the locomotive was forty years old. It still worked like new. Three times each day it pulled the antique passenger cars over the redwood-covered mountain.

_____

_____

_____

4. Mary had two young children to support. She wanted to find a job. As soon as she finished two years of college.

_____

_____

_____

5. After his son was born but before his daughter was born. Jim was in an accident in which his back was broken. For more than a year he was unable to work.

_____

_____

_____

**73**

Have your sentences checked.

**Phrase Fragments**

A phrase—a meaningful group of words without a subject and a verb—or a series of phrases must always be a part of a sentence. Either a phrase or series of phrases mistakenly placed by itself as if it were a sentence is a *sentence fragment* that should be corrected.

*Examples*

| WRONG | CORRECTED |
|---|---|
| The new subdivision will be located across the river. *On the Sullivan Ranch property.* | The new subdivision will be located across the river *on the Sullivan Ranch Property.* |
| Fred was in the library. *Working on a research paper.* | Fred was in the library, *working on a research paper.* |
| She quit. *Smoking tobacco.* But she didn't stop drinking bourbon. | She quit *smoking tobacco,* but she didn't stop drinking bourbon. |
| John hitchhiked to Portland. *To find a job.* | John hitchhiked to Portland *to find a job.* |
| She had a dog. *A large English sheepdog that loved ice cream.* | She had a dog, *a large English sheepdog that loved ice cream.* |
| The bridge fell. *On the train underneath it.* | The bridge fell *on the train underneath it.* |
| *Seeing the test score. Made him panicky.* | *Seeing the test score made him panicky.* |

**EXERCISE 21**

First, underline the *phrase fragment*; next correct the fragment either by connecting it to the sentence in front of it or by rewriting the fragment to form a complete sentence. Punctuate each sentence correctly.

1. They continued on their hike. Undefeated by the rain.

_____

_____

_____

2. He wanted to do his homework. After the movie.

_____

_____

_____

74

3. The widow built a home on the edge of the mountain lake. A huge stone castle resembling a Viking fortress.

_____

_____

4. She wanted the opportunity. To show her father that she could handle the responsibility.

_____

_____

_____

5. Brad continued. Teasing his little sister in spite of his mother's repeated orders to stop.

_____

_____

_____

6. The old pine tree fell. Crashing into the cabin roof.

_____

_____

_____

7. The President made his decision. Not to run for re-election.

_____

_____

_____

8. He took the job. With the understanding that he would not get a vacation the first year.

_____

_____

_____

9. The job provided a challenge. More of a challenge than he expected.

_____

_____

_____

10. The antique porcelain vase lay on the floor. Broken into dozens of tiny pieces. The rosewood stand. However, was unbroken.

**75**

_____

_____

_____

Some of the following pairs contain *sentence fragments*. Write *CORRECT* after each pair in which both word groups are complete sentences; correct any fragment *by combining it* with the complete sentence that accompanies it. Each sentence must be properly punctuated. (Answers on page 87)

1. Hundreds of homes were damaged when the ammunition train exploded. A senseless tragedy.

_____

_____

_____

2. The literature class was assigned to read seven books. Some students found seven too many.

_____

_____

_____

3. The team spirit has been very high since she began playing third base. Because she is always able to pep up the rest of the team with her laughter, jokes, and chatter.

_____

_____

_____

4. The trouble with Jordon's theory is that he has failed to take human nature into account. Unfortunately, people do not always act predictably.

_____

_____

_____

5. Too many students fail college courses during their first semester. Either because of poor preparation or study habits.

_____

_____

_____

Have your work checked.

## Run-on Sentence and Comma Splices

### What Is a Run-on Sentence?

Many instructors assume that students who do not correct *run-on sentences* are poor writers. The *run-on sentence* consists of two or more independent clauses, or sentences, that have been connected *without any punctuation*. Thus, the reader who sees two independent clauses that have been carelessly fused is often confused by the faulty construction and is forced to reread them, trying to make sense out of run-together ideas.

*Examples*

> Mary had a little lamb she sold it to the butcher.
>
> He never seems to answer questions he always counters with questions of his own.

### What Is a Comma Splice?

A *comma splice* is another kind of faulty connection in which two independent clauses, or sentences, are mistakenly joined *with a comma but no conjunction*. In a comma splice, the comma is inserted between the two independent clauses, but the conjunction is forgotten—a serious writing mistake.

*Examples*

> Mary had a little lamb, she sold it to the butcher.
>
> He never seems to answer questions, he always counters with questions of his own.

### Correcting Run-ons and Comma Splices

Run-on and comma-splice errors may be corrected by *six* methods. The method you choose will depend upon what appears to be best in a particular situation and your personal preference.

1. **Use a semicolon:**

> (Run-on error) The hawk swooped down upon the ***mouse she*** then flew back to her nest.
>
> (comma-splice error) The hawk swooped down upon the mouse, she then flew back to her nest.
>
> (revised) The hawk swooped down upon the mouse; she then flew back to her nest.

The independent clauses are correctly joined by a *semicolon* in the revision. This method is particularly effective when the clauses to be connected are closely related, but indiscriminate use of the semicolon should be avoided.

2. **Use a comma and its accompanying conjunction:**

> (run-on error) The famous band played a three-hour Halloween ***concert most*** of the audience thought it was their best concert in years.
>
> (comma-splice error) The famous band played a three-hour Halloween concert, most of the audience thought it was their best concert in years.
>
> (revised) The famous band played a three-hour Halloween concert, ***and*** most of the audience thought it was their best concert in years.

Be careful! Many students remember to use the comma, but they forget to place a conjunction after it. (The most commonly used conjunctions are *and, but,* and *or.*)

### 3. Incorporate in an independent clause:

(run-on error) The killer in the movie *Hush, Hush, Sweet Charlotte* chopped off the man's **hand then** she chopped off his head.

(comma-splice error) The killer in the movie *Hush, Hush, Sweet Charlotte* chopped off the man's hand, then she chopped off his head.

(revised) The killer in the movie *Hush, Hush, Sweet Charlotte* chopped off the man's hand *and then chopped off his head.*

(revised) The killer in the movies *Hush, Hush, Sweet Charlotte* chopped off the man's hand, *then his head.*

(revised) The killer in the movie *Hush, Hush, Sweet Carlotte* chopped off the man's hand *and head.*

All three of the above revisions are correct. In each case the second independent clause has been shortened, first, by omitting the subject, second, by leaving out both the subject and predicate and finally, by condensing the independent clause to a compound direct object.

### 4. Construct a complex sentence:

(run-on error) Mr. Herder shocked the small ***town he*** moved in with Jennie and Josie.

(comma-splice error) Mr. Herder shocked the small town, he moved in with Jennie and Josie.

(revised) When Mr. Herder moved in with Jennie and Josie, he shocked the small town.

(revised) Mr. Herder, who moved in with Jennie and Josie, shocked the small town.

(revised) Mr. Herder shocked the small town when he moved in with Jennie and Josie.

Each of the revisions above is correct. The complex sentence is a good option to use when you want to *subordinate* one of the independent clauses in the comma splice. The main idea in the above revisions is emphasized by placing it in an independent clause—Mr. Herder shocked the town. The subordinate idea—that he moved in with Jennie and Josie—is de-emphasized by placing it in the dependent clause. (Study the punctuation in each revision.)

### 5. Use a semicolon and a conjunctive adverb:

(run-on error) As the night wore on, they became less and less interested in fishing by ***flashlight they*** were freezing.

(comma-splice error) As the night wore on, they became less and less interested in fishing by flashlight, they were freezing.

(revised) As the night wore on, they became less and less interested in fishing by flashlight*; moreover*, they were freezing.

The *conjunctive adverb* makes the logical connection between the two independent clauses clear—the ideas are clearly *coordinated*.

Always punctuate *conjunctive adverbs* correctly. Whenever two independent clauses (or two sentences) are connected with a conjunctive adverb, a semicolon should be placed

**78**

*in front* of the conjunctive adverb, and usually a comma should be placed *after* it. Often a student will make the mistake of forgetting the semicolon or using just a comma when the stronger semicolon is needed.

Run-on-Error—

The new model will cost **more however,** new features will make it a better product.

Comma-splice Error—

The new model will cost more, however, new features will make it a better product.

Revised—

The new model will cost more; **however,** new features will make it a better product.

6. **Make two sentences:**

(run-on error) Jeff and Jennie Patton committed suicide by driving their old car into the Mississippi **River thus,** they died with dignity.

(comma splice) Jeff and Jennie Patton committed suicide by driving their old car into the Mississippi River, thus, they died with dignity.

(revised) Jeff and Jennie Patton committed suicide by driving their old car into the Mississippi River. **Thus, they died with dignity.**

In the above example, dividing the faulty sentence into two sentences works well because the second sentence expresses an idea that is not easily coordinated or subordinated with the idea in the first sentence. This method of correction is not advisable if the division creates short, choppy sentences.

---

NOTE: A *comma splice* is sometimes acceptable in a sentence containing a series of three or more independent clauses. In such cases the *last two* independent clauses must be joined with a conjunction.

*Example*

The bargain was made, the date was set, *and* the contract could not be altered.

He saw the problem, he weighed the danger, *but* he decided to go ahead with the project.

---

**EXERCISE 23**

Write *definitions* for the following terms: (Answers on page 88)

1. Sentence fragment

**79**

2. Run-on sentence

3. Comma-splice

_____

_____

## EXERCISE 24

Correct each *run-on* or *comma-splice* error. Use a variety of methods.

1. Six were aboard the yacht when it arrived in Hawaii only five were aboard when it departed.

_____

_____

_____

2. The road became too steep for the car to continue ahead, therefore, we walked up the narrow road to the fire tower.

_____

_____

_____

3. Whatever else one may say about him, Phillipe was a game fighter he never considered quitting while he could stand.

_____

_____

_____

4. The thunder and lightning grew worse, the dog became frightened he crawled under the bed.

_____

_____

_____

**80** 5. Logging trucks are unbelievably powerful they can travel much faster than one would think, they are, however, more difficult to stop than one would think, too.

_____

_____

_____

Have your revisions checked.

# Unit Two Practice Test

This test is just like the *Unit Two Posttest* that you must take after completing the work in this unit. If you pass *all three parts* of this test, ask your instructor for the *Unit Two Posttest*. If you do not pass one or more of the parts, study the test items missed and then restudy the appropriate lesson or lessons before taking the Unit Two Posttest. ANSWERS ON PAGE 88. *The following items must be checked by your instructor*: 1-2, 4-5, 8-9, 11, 13-14, 17, 19-25.

| **Passing Scores** | **Your Scores** |
|---|---|
| Part One - 24 points | Part One _____ (28 pts. possible) |
| Part Two - 40 points | Part Two _____ (44 pts. possible) |
| Part Three - 24 points | Part Three _____ (28 pts. possible) |

**PART ONE: LESSON ONE (4 points each)**

1. Define the term *compound sentence*.

   _____

   _____

2. Write a *compound sentence*, using *but* for a *conjunction*. Punctuate the sentence correctly.

   _____

   _____

   _____

3. (Circle the correct *conjunction*.) Before the next meeting John is supposed to poll the faculty, (*and, but, for*) Marie is supposed to survey the class presidents.

4. Write a *compound sentence*, using only a *semicolon* for a *connector*. (Do *not* use a *conjunctive adverb*.)

   _____

   _____

   _____

5. Write a *compound sentence*, using *consequently* as a *conjunctive adverb*. Punctuate the sentence correctly.

   _____

   _____

   _____

6. (Circle the correct *conjunctive adverb*.) In the past, legislative plans to control strip mining were usually defeated; (*therefore, however, in addition*), this week the House voted for a series of proposals that call for reclaiming land strip-mined in the future and restoring land strip-mined in the past.

7. (Circle the letter of the correct answer.) The italicized word in the following sentence is used as
   a. an INTRODUCTORY TRANSITIONAL WORD OR PHRASE
   b. an INTERRUPTING TRANSITIONAL WORD OR PHRASE
   c. a CONJUNCTIVE ADVERB

   The present draft of the law states that a federal police agency could apply for an electronic surveillance permit if it appeared that a suspect were "engaging in secret activities dangerous to national security"; *however*, civil liberties forces are expected to oppose the law.

## PART TWO: LESSON TWO (4 points each)

8. Define the term *phrase*.

   _____

   _____

9. Define the term *clause*.

   _____

   _____

10. (Circle the letter of the correct answer.) The following word groups are
    a. INDEPENDENT CLAUSES
    b. DEPENDENT CLAUSES
    c. PHRASES
    d. SIGNAL WORDS FOR DEPENDENT CLAUSES

    *after the earthquake*
    *late in the evening*
    *turning the corner*
    *powered by a gas turbine*

11. Add a *signal word or phrase* that will convert the following group of words to a *dependent clause*.

    two scripts for the science-fiction thriller were rejected by Paramount.

12. Underline each of the *dependent clauses* in the following sentence. (2 or 3 dependent clauses)

    The light-beam weapon, which is focused and aimed by magnetic mirrors, uses an enormous quantity of energy that is kept in a tight beam by injecting heavy protons.

13. The sentence below is a *compound sentence*. Convert it to a *complex-sentence* by using a *signal word or phrase* to subordinate one of the independent clauses. Punctuate the sentence correctly.

    Death ray weapons are being developed by the superpowers, and they will make anti-ballistic missiles obsolete.

**82**

   _____

   _____

   _____

14. Write a *complex sentence* in which the independent clause is *followed* by a dependent clause. Punctuate the sentence correctly.

_____

_____

_____

15. Circle the letter of the correctly punctuated sentence.
    a. The opera *Aida*, which Betty and George had seen three times, was sold out three months in advance.
    b. The opera *Aida*, which Betty and George had seen three times was sold out three months in advance.
    c. The opera *Aida* which Betty and Bill had seen three times was sold out three months in advance.

16. Which sentence is a *compound-complex* sentence? (Circle the correct letter.)
    a. When the rain finally stopped, no one wanted to leave the warm cabin.
    b. The supersonic fighter plane, which is manufactured in France, is in great demand, and most experts think it is one of the best planes of its type in the world.
    c. Before beginning the new job, Shirley will take a refresher course in shorthand because she has not practiced it since she was a high school senior.

17. Write a *compound-complex* sentence. Punctuate the sentence correctly.

_____

_____

_____

18. (Punctuate the following sentence correctly.) Even though the records show that sales have increased profits are down but they should begin to rise when the new cost-cutting computer system is introduced.

## PART THREE: LESSON THREE (4 points each)

19. Define the term *sentence fragment*.

_____

_____

20. Underline the *dependent clause fragment*, and then correct it.
    The researcher found that women are marrying later and postponing having children. Because the women want to work more than they want to be mothers. More women are remaining single, too.

_____

_____

_____

_____

**83**

21. Underline the *phrase fragment* and then correct it.

    The former professor was convicted in Baltimore on charges of espionage, theft, and conspiracy. For stealing and selling to Soviet agents top-secret documents.

    _____

    _____

    _____

22. Define the term *run-on sentence*. _____

    _____

23. (Correct each *run-on* error.) An unbelievable amount of dust clogged the filter as a result, the motor was overheating.

    _____

    _____

    _____

24. Define the term *comma splice*.

    _____

    _____

25. (Correct the *comma-splice* error.) Military experts are worried that one of the superpowers will launch a doomsday nuclear attack against one of the other superpowers, the attacking nation might base its decision to launch a first-strike on the fear that it would have no chance to launch a return attack if it were attacked first.

    _____

    _____

    _____

    _____

    _____

# Answers for Unit Two Exercises

**Exercise 1 (page 48)**

1. A compound sentence is two or more closely related simple sentences that are connected.
2. A compound sentence is two or more closely related independent clauses that are connected.

**Exercise 2 (page 49)**

Your answers will vary; have your sentences checked.

**Exercise 3 (page 51)**

1. yet        6. and
2. but        7. for
3. but        8. yet
4. or         9. or
5. but       10. but

**Exercise 4 (page 52)**

1. A compound sentence is two or more closely related simple sentences that are connected.
2. A compound sentence is two or more closely related independent clauses that are connected.

**Exercise 5 (page 52)**

Your answers will vary: have your sentences checked.

**Exercise 6 (page 54)**

1. A compound sentence is two or more closely related simple sentences that are connected.
2. A compound sentence is two or more closely related independent clauses that are connected.

**Exercise 7 (page 54)**

Your answers will vary: have your sentences checked.

**Exercise 8 (page 56)**

1. ; therefore,    ; thus,    ; consequently,
2. ; however,    ; nevertheless,
3. ; therefore,    ; thus,    ; consequently,
4. ; moreover,    ; furthermore,    ; in addition,    ; consequently,
5. ; moreover,    furthermore,    ; in addition,    ; however,
6. ; however,    ; nevertheless,    ; of course,
7. ; however,    ; nevertheless,
8. ; unfortunately,    ; however,
9. ; for instance,    ; for example,
10. ; therefore,    ; thus,    ; consequently,

**Exercise 9 (page 57)**

A   1. For example,
A   2. Moreover,
C   3. ; however,
B,B 4. , to be sure, . . . , however,
C   5. ; in fact,

85

**Exercise 10 (page 60)**

Your answers will vary; have your work checked.

**Exercise 11 (page 62)**

1. phrase
2. dependent clause
3. signal phrase
4. independent clause
5. dependent clause
6. phrase
7. dependent clause
8. independent clause
9. signal word
10. dependent clause
11. independent clause
12. phrase
13. signal phrase
14. phrase
15. signal word
16. dependent clause
17. phrase
18. independent clause
19. dependent clause
20. signal word

**Exercise 12 (page 63)**

Your answers will vary; have your work checked.

**Exercise 13 (page 64)**

1. *Although his friends are corrupt*, he insists *that his hands are clean.*
2. He was not afraid of the growling dog *because he had his lucky coin in his pocket.*
3. Mayor Jones, *whom everyone considered a liar*, stated *that he would not seek another term.*
4. *Since he celebrated his fortieth birthday*, he has begun to spend more time with his family.
5. The dress was the one *that she had been hoping to find on sale.*

**Exercise 14 (page 64)**

1. Ideas are coordinated in a compound sentence when two or more independent clauses (simple sentences) are joined by a connector.
2. Answers vary; have your work checked.
3. An idea is subordinated in a complex sentence by placing it in the dependent clause.
4. Answers vary; have your work checked.

**Exercise 15 (page 65)**

Your answers will vary; have your work checked.

**Exercise 16 (page 67)**

Your answers will vary; have your work checked.

**Exercise 17 (page 68)**

1. Although the weather forecast predicted rain , the sky was clear and blue.
2. The sky was dark and threatening although the forecast called for clear skies.
3. The parking lot was always full when classes started in the fall.
4. When the semester was almost over , there were many empty parking spaces.
5. The pants that she purchased Saturday were marked down for a sale on Monday.
6. The blazer which she thought about during her coffee break was not marked down.
7. Ralph knew that he had made a mistake , that he had made a terrible mistake.
8. As far as they could tell after consulting several experts , no tidal wave would follow the small quake.
9. As predicted , Arnold Fletcher , who had conducted the civic orchestra for ten years , wanted to retire at the end of the spring concert series.
10. The settler who built the cabin never did farm the land after clearing it.

**Exercise 18 (page 69)**

Your answers will vary; have your work checked.

**Exercise 19 (page 70)**

1. When we got home , her father was waiting at the front door.
2. While the snow was falling , no traffic moved.
3. no punctuation
4. Jan and Ricky , when they were much younger , were always in trouble.
5. She kept entering million dollar contests , but she never won.
6. no punctuation
7. no punctuation
8. When our group was asked for our report , we could only laugh.
9. Although it was fall , everyone in class seemed to have spring fever.
10. Geometry , which is not my favorite subject , is the only class I hate to attend.
11. no punctuation
12. Avery Anderson , who delivers our mail , is getting married next Sunday.
13. However , the automobile was not for sale.
14. The frightened horse , moreover , stepped on the fallen rider.
15. Furthermore , the yelling grooms made the horse more excited , and he ran into the side of the judge's car.
16. Jaguars , which I like better than Corvettes , are fine sport cars.
17. Joe is prejudiced against women ; he thinks they are incapable of being anything but mothers.
18. While we were in Ireland last year , it rained and rained and rained.
19. American River canoe trips produce sore muscles , sunburned skin , and many happy memories.
20. We knew , of course , that exploring caves was dangerous ; nevertheless , we entered the cave without food , rope , or flashlights.
21. no punctuation
22. Chuck , a guy we met at the bottom of the canyon , and a few other people were about ten minutes behind us.
23. no punctuation
24. When Jane and I hiked closer to the falls , the noise became so loud that we had to scream to hear one another although we were only ten feet apart.
25. Pro-abortion arguments have been based on the premise that pregnant women should have the final say , that men have too long made these decisions from their own perspective , for men are not the ones who must actually bear the babies.

**Exercise 20 (page 73)**

Your answers will vary; have your work checked.

**Exercise 21 (page 74)**

Your answers will vary; have your work checked.

**Exercise 22 (page 76)**

1. Hundreds of homes were damaged, a senseless tragedy, when the ammunition train exploded.

-or-

Hundreds of homes were damaged when the ammunition train exploded, a senseless tragedy.
2. correct

3. The team spirit has been very high since she began playing third base because she is always able to pep up the rest of the team with her laughter, jokes, and chatter.

-or-

Because she is always able to pep up the rest of the team with her laughter, jokes, and chatter, the team spirit has been very high since she began playing third base.

4. correct

5. Too many students fail college courses during their first semester, either because of poor preparation or study habits.

-or-

Either because of poor preparation or study habits, too many students fail college courses during their first semester.

**Exercise 23 (page 79)**

1. A sentence fragment is a part of a sentence punctuated as if it were a complete sentence.

2. A run-on sentence consists of two or more independent clauses, or sentences, that have been connected without any punctuation.

3. A comma splice consists of two or more independent clauses, or sentences, that have been connected with a comma but no conjunction.

**Exercise 24 (page 80)**

Your answers will vary; have your work checked.

**Unit Two Practice Test (page 81)**

1-2. Instructor checks

3. and

4-5. Instructor checks

6. however

7. c

8-9. Instructor checks

10. c

11. Instructor checks

12. The light-beam weapon, *which is focused and aimed by magnetic mirrors*, uses an enormous quantity of energy *that is kept in a tight beam    by injecting heavy protons.*

13-14. Instructor checks

15. a

16. b

17. Instructor checks

18. Even though the records show that sales have increased , profits are down , but they should begin to rise when the new cost-cutting computer system is introduced.

19-25. Instructor checks

# UNIT THREE
## Narrative and Descriptive Writing

## *Objectives*

After completing this unit, you will be able to

1. write interesting *narration.*
2. identify *first, second,* and *third person.*
3. define and demonstrate *chronological (time) ordering.*
4. write interesting *description.*
5. *combine* narrative and descriptive writing.

# 3

You have successfully completed Units One and Two, and you are ready to begin a new unit, but do not forget what you have learned. These units reviewed basic sentence structure so you would be able to write effective sentences in subsequent units. Occasionally you should review sections of Units One and Two to refresh your knowledge. Also, you should have your dictionary with you every time you write. No instructor expects your writing to be perfect, but every instructor wants you to **review, consult, correct,** and **revise**—to make your writing as nearly perfect as possible.

Unit Three presents two common kinds of writing: **Narrative** and **Descriptive**. Although actually separate terms, they appear together so commonly that most writers consider *narrative-descriptive* writing one term. Though the term might be new to you, you are far more familiar with this type of writing than you might imagine. In fact, it is very likely that you have used this technique recently because almost every letter you write employs the narrative and descriptive technique.

Most important, however, is that you will use narrative-descriptive writing in some classes where you are asked to submit reports as a part of the course requirements. In addition to using this method in reports, you will also have opportunities to write narration and description in papers you develop for English, history, psychology, and other academic classes. In an anecdotal paragraph, for instance, you will use narration and description as you make a point by explaining what happened to you or someone else. As you study this unit, you will discover why this type of writing has been a favorite of both instructors and students; it can be both fun to write and rewarding to read.

## LESSON ONE—What Is a Narrative?

*Narrative* is the easiest type of writing for most beginning composition students because it tells a story. Everyone gives many narratives daily. When a child comes home from school and excitedly tells a family member what happened at school, that child is delivering a narrative. The same is true of the worker who returns home after work and tells the family about an incident which occurred on the job that day. When these same stories are written, they are still narratives. A common form of written narrative with which you are undoubtedly familiar is the personal letter. But think for a moment about a personal letter, and you will realize that most such letters include narratives of many different incidents, not just one. Nevertheless, personal letters are narratives, even though they include numerous accounts. Notice how different incidents are narrated in the following letter.

The Gilbertese people gave us a nice welcome on Fanning Island. At first, it seemed to be a great staring contest, but the natives are generous, fun-loving people, and we soon had enjoyed many good experiences with them. There is one small village of about 385 people (260 are children), and it did not take long for us to become familiar with most of them. Many spoke English well enough to carry on good conversations. We fished, snorkeled, ate, sang and danced with the natives, and learned much information about the copra plantation and Fanning Island from the managers, an English couple who were the only Europeans living on the island. After living native style for two weeks (or I should say developing some native habits like drinking toti and eating without utensils but refusing to eat raw fish straight out of the skin) we reluctantly left our peaceful anchorage in the lagoon. We waved good-bye to our friends standing on the reef, thinking of all our happy experiences we had shared with them. It was sad to leave friends, but we were looking forward to many more on Christmas Island.

We had a nice three-day sail to Christmas Island—actually it was a much easier beat than we had expected. This atoll is very similar to Fanning Island but larger, not as pretty, and much more influenced by Western civilization due to war activities (much building was done for the testing of the hydrogen bomb—all has been left behind to rust and decay and really is an unsightly mess). We noticed this influence in the people there and found ourselves much more attracted to the unspoiled atmosphere on Fanning. We did, however, have some nice crayfish hunts on the reefs under lantern light. Ninety-five was the total catch, and did we ever have a good feast! Some of these creatures grow to lengths of three feet and are similar in looks and taste to our lobster.

Although this is only a small portion of a much longer letter, you can easily see that it relates a series of impressions and events. The letter is, nevertheless, organized. *The writer uses the first paragraph to tell about the experiences on Fanning Island.* The narration of these events is arranged so that it proceeds from the sail to get there to the farewell from that island. *The second paragraph narrates the author's impressions of Christmas Island.* This paragraph has been organized differently because the author's main objective is to compare and contrast Christmas Island with Fanning Island. She does, however, tell about one specific incident—a crayfish hunt. A writer's job—your job—in any narrative or descriptive writing is generally the same: to relate **interesting details** in an **organized composition.**

**92**

### Person

All of your narratives will be written in either first, second, or third person, depending on your purpose and your audience. A **first-person narrative** is characterized by use of the pronouns *I, me,* and *we.*

*Examples—*

> *I* was amazed to see . . .
> The strange man walked toward *me* . . .
> *We* were disappointed to find . . .

In **second-person narrative** the reader is referred to by *name* or by the use of the pronoun **you**.

*Examples—*

> *John, you* can't believe how parched the countryside was during the drought.
> Upon entering the castle, *you* will see . . .

Second-person narrative should be avoided in academic writing. Instructors believe that it is suitable only for personal correspondence or for talks and speeches where the author can maintain eye contact with the audience.

*Second person narrative should be avoided . . .*

In **third-person narrative**, people, places, and events are referred to objectively by *name* or *description*, and the only pronouns that appear frequently are *he, she, it,* and *they*.

**93**

*Examples—*

> *The group* was disappointed to find . . .
> *The countryside* was parched during the drought . . .
> *Harriett* knew that . . .
> *She* hunted crayfish . . .
> *It* came running . . .

The distinction between first, second, and third person may not seem great to you at this point, but most instructors will insist that you choose either *first* or *third* person and then use it consistently through whatever you are writing. They will not want you to use second person, and they will not want you to switch from the use of one person to another as you might in a more casual narrative, such as a letter. Study the following examples; they provide longer examples of first and third-person writing.

**First Person**

Knowing little about the dangers involved, I climbed on my half-submerged log and proceeded to row with homemade paddles from one island to the next. The distance between was about two miles, but I failed to consider the fact that I was crossing open ocean water. Luckily, the water and weather were quite calm! Halfway between the islands, however, I was reminded that my legs hung into the water below the log when I saw a number of fins coming toward me. Thinking of the sharks behind me and paddling furiously toward the island I had left, I began a short but hopeless race. I had covered no more than fifty feet when the great finned creatures were upon me. One brushed against the log while another brushed my leg. Expecting to feel teeth in my leg at any moment, I increased my paddling. Suddenly, the threatening fish began to leap completely out of the water, obviously enjoying playing "cat and mouse" with their noon meal. Just as suddenly, I realized that sharks do not jump out of the water. The realization that I was surrounded by a group of playful porpoises flooded my heart with happiness.

**Third Person**

Knowing little about the danger involved, Bob climbed on his half-submerged log and proceeded to row with homemade paddles from one island to the next. The distance between the islands was about two miles, but he failed to consider the fact that he was crossing open ocean water. Luckily, the water and weather were quite calm! Halfway between the islands, however, Bob was reminded that his legs hung into the water below the log when he saw a number of fins coming toward him. Thinking of the sharks behind him and paddling furiously toward the island he had left, he began a short but hopeless race. He had covered no more than fifty feet when the giant finned creatures were upon him. One brushed against the log while another brushed his leg. Expecting to feel teeth in his leg at any moment, he increased his paddling. Suddenly, the threatening fish began to leap completely out of the water, obviously enjoying playing "cat and mouse" with their noon meal. Just as suddenly, Bob realized that sharks do not jump out of the water. The realization that he was surrounded by a group of playful porpoises flooded his heart with happiness.

Newspapers include extensive first and third-person narratives every day. The news item which tells about an accident will almost always be in third person (unless the reporter was involved in the accident he is reporting). An article in which the reporter tells how he was treated by the mob in a demonstration would be in first person. Some magazines deliberately attempt to present a balance of first and third-person narratives; others, such as travel magazines, print first-person accounts almost exclusively when they use narratives.

A *primary concern* you must face when you write any narrative is whether to make your story *real* or *invented*. If you invent a story, your narrative will be called **fiction**, but it is still narrative. A *second concern* for the narrative writer is to *establish a setting* early

94

in the story. Somehow, you must let your reader know *where* and *when* the event occurred so he can visualize what happened. The *third concern* is to be sure you tell *what* action is taking place and *who* is involved in it.

**EXERCISE 1**

1. List the three primary concerns of the narrative writer.

   a)

   b)

   c)

2. Which pronouns are most often used in third-person narratives?

   a)                b)                c)                d)

3. Which pronouns are most commonly used in first-person narratives?

   a)                b)                c)

4. List three common places you might find narratives in your daily life.

   a)                b)  ,            c)

5. The two paragraphs of the letter appearing in this lesson are presented in which person?

   Have your work checked.

**How Long Is a Narrative?**

The *length* of a narrative varies tremendously. Novels and narrative non-fiction books are hundreds of pages long. The narrative accounts published in magazines are typically between five and ten typed pages in length. By contrast, the narratives you write for this book will be much shorter. Consider, for example, a narrative of only one paragraph. Although you may want to tell about an entire trip, you are limited to only one incident in a single paragraph. For instance, if you wrote about your trip to Disneyworld, you could not tell about the whole trip in one paragraph. Perhaps you could only tell about your experience riding *Space Mountain*—and that would be a long paragraph.

Read the following paragraph closely:

> My first several nights out on patrol were very uneventful. None of the other K-9 patrols had made any enemy contact, and I was overwhelmed by a great feeling of security on my fourth night. My mind wandered as I dreamed of what people were doing back in the United States. Suddenly, with a great surge, Duke lunged forward, alerting me to the presence of an intruder. Through the corner of my eye, I saw the shadow of an individual about twenty-five yards to my left. I challenged the intruder as specified under MAC-V Rules of Engagement. I received no acknowledgement from the intruder so I fired on him with my AR-15. I cautiously moved forward to the position where I had last seen the intruder. To my surprise, a man lay very still and dead on the ground.

Wisely, the writer of this paragraph did not attempt to tell about his entire patrol that night. He could have told about reporting for duty, getting his orders for the night, finding and checking over his dog, and walking in the dark to his station. However, he limited himself, and the paragraph is more effective because of the limiting. Equally tempting in a situation such as this is the continuation of the story. If you get "carried away" with the story, you may find yourself going on and on. Here, the writer deliberately avoided telling what he did after he found the dead man. All discussion of how the writer felt, what the dog did, and what action was taken by the military commander belongs in subsequent paragraphs.

## What to Write About?

You can write a narrative about any experience you have had, but your most memorable experiences will be the best to write about since they will be the most interesting to your reader. Consider the following list of topics as you search for possible events to narrate:

1. my first date
2. my first day on the job
3. my accident
4. the time I was really embarrassed
5. the experience I can't forget
6. the time I went rafting down the river
7. the night I learned what fear was
8. what I did when I locked myself out
9. why I enjoyed the party
10. my experiences at registration
11. others _____

_____

_____

## EXERCISE 2

1. Pick two topics from the list above. (Your own are fine.)

   a) _____

   b) _____

2. In two sentences, tell about a small part of one topic that you could develop into a paragraph.

**96**

_____

_____

_____

_____

Before you begin developing one of your topics into a full-length paragraph, consider how you will communicate to your reader what you are attempting to say. Writers all too frequently lose the reader with the first sentence because they neglect to include a **purpose sentence.** This sentence must inform your reader of your purpose in writing, without being overbearing. Beginning with *"I am going to tell you about . . ."* or *"My purpose is . . ."* will almost certainly make your paragraph sound childish; therefore, a more subtle approach must be found. *A better technique is to begin with a sentence that introduces the subject and draws attention to a particular aspect of it at the same time.* Carefully read the following paragraph. Notice that the writer is only concerned with telling about the *"inspiring place"* she found in the mountains.

I discovered the most beautiful, inspiring place in my world once while I was hiking in the mountains during a summer rainstorm. Gradually, I had become aware of a loud, roaring sound coming from deep within the canyon ahead. I knew at once that when I got to the bottom I would find a swelling stream rushing along its banks. It was only a few minutes later that my guess became reality. There I was, standing face to face with the most beautiful series of intricately carved waterfalls I had ever seen. The rain had begun to subside, and I had an uncontrollable urge to strip to the skin and bathe in the churning waters. Soon, I was romping and splashing in the icy stream; for a minute, I stood beneath one of the many waterfalls and received an invigorating, natural shower. I have never been to a place that gave me such a voluptuous, lusty feeling. It is a place that I have returned to uncountable times, feeling just as excited as when I accidentally stumbled onto it several years ago.

**EXERCISE 3**

Using *first person*, write a **narrative paragraph** on one of the topics in Exercise 2. Make sure you describe the incident completely, but do not cover more than one incident. Note! Your paragraph can narrate a real or imaginary incident.

97

_____

_____

_____

_____

_____

_____

_____

_____

_____

_____

_____

_____

_____

_____

_____

_____

_____

_____

_____

_____

## EXERCISE 4

Now take the same event you told about in the last exercise and convert it into a *third-person* narrative paragraph.

_____

_____

_____

99

Have your work checked.

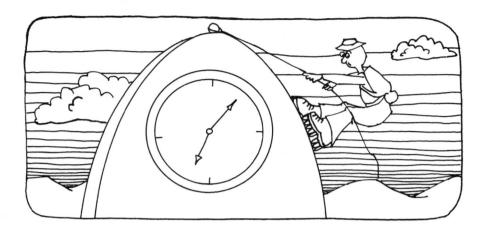

## Ordering for Narrative Writing

To avoid producing a narrative that leaves your reader confused, you must give order to your writing. For a narrative, the most commonly employed technique of ordering is **time** (chronological) **ordering**. There are other types, of course, but they are special types which are used infrequently so you need not be concerned with them at this point.

Chronological ordering requires you to tell what happened *first, second, third, and so on*. By using time ordering, you tell your tale so that your reader becomes aware of passing time. Notice how the authors of the following paragraphs have told their stories:

### 1

My experiences during my first day in Naples will never be forgotten. The reason my memory is so vivid, I believe, is that I had shore patrol. And if anything left a bad taste in my mouth, it was playing ''cop'' with two thousand sailors in a foreign port. My duties started with listening to a lecture by one of the ''hardhats'' (permanent shore patrol stationed in that town). His talk was short and centered around one sentence: ''If my mother were Italian, I wouldn't turn my back on her!'' This made me worry about what to expect during a day that already belonged to the Lord's adversary. As it turned out, I was assigned a partner and told to keep all sailors out of a part of town that could only be called ''different.'' What an experience—within the first couple of hours we were rolled by a herd of kids, approximately eight to ten years old. To this gang, my partner lost his wallet. After lunch, for which I paid, I enjoyed the thrill of being violently attacked by a ''lady of the street.'' She recognized me for what I was—a threat to her livelihood. And this upset her so much that she felt obligated to follow me nearly a block, pounding my more exposed parts with her left foot and screaming the only English words she knew—words harsh even to a sailor's ears. And that was the way the remainder of the day went, and also the night: threats from Communists in search of anti-American propaganda and a perpetual stream of fights in need of mediation. Naples, Italy, impressed itself on my mind as though it were a child working with his first woodburning set.

The misty, clinging monsoon season rain diffused and reflected the yellowish glare of the descending circle of parachute flares which always encircled Pleiku Air Base after dark. The rays of a movie projector danced in spasmodic beams of color through the foggy, moist air onto the deteriorated surface of an outdoor movie screen. The viewers, apparently indifferent to the weather, sat in a forward leaning position on crude benches with no backs. Their attire was mostly the olive drab of work uniforms or the mottled greens of jungle fatigues with an occasional blotch of color from a PX sport shirt. There was little movement as though this would somehow slow down the saturation process. The audience of about one hundred contained a mixture of ranks and ages that, for the time being, were meaningless as each escaped in his own way into the two-dimensional fantasy before him. I was fairly well hidden behind the last row, smugly enjoying two recent acquisitions: a folding lawn chair and a large black umbrella. At about 2100, reality was announced to everyone abruptly by two incoming mortar rounds exploding just behind the movie screen. After a mad rush for the nearest bunker, I found myself seated next to a young airman in the dark, dank bowels of the sand-bag igloo shielding us from what now was a full-fledged rocket and mortar attack. The young man kept glancing at me furtively as if he wanted to ask me something but couldn't bring himself to do it. Playing my role as a senior non-commissioned officer, I squinted my eyes and took a deep drag on a rather bent cigarette letting the smoke casually curl out through my nose. It was as close as I could come to a look somewhere between John Wayne and Charles Bronson. I was thinking of tough, but reassuring replies to counteract any signs of hysteria. He finally looked me right in the eyes. "Sergeant," he said rather curtly, "Your umbrella is poking me in the ribs, your folding chair is blocking the exit, and I'll trade you some beer for a puff on that cigarette." As he savored the last few puffs on my cigarette, I relocated my umbrella and chair and finished off his beer, feeling quite comfortable as a normal, imperfect three-dimensional human being.

The two paragraphs above are effective because they are narrated in the time order in which they happened. This is known as **natural time order** or **chronological order.** The first writer writes, "After lunch, for which I paid, I enjoyed the thrill of being violently attacked by a 'lady of the street.'" This one sentence shows natural time order as it tells that the writer had lunch, then paid for lunch, and then was attacked. Similarly, the second paragraph clearly shows natural time order as the writer tells of his experiences in a war situation.

## EXERCISE 5

Write one narrative paragraph in which you use **chronological** (time) **ordering**. Also, use at least three different types of sentence constructions studied in Units One and Two. Make certain your spelling, punctuation, and sentence structure are correct.

**101**

**102**

Have your worked checked.

# LESSON TWO—Description

**Narration** and **description** go together like sailboats and wind. Narrative writing can stand alone just as a sailboat can exist without wind, but both are very unimpressive without their counterparts. Without wind, a sailboat is a dead "thing" which merely bobs uncomfortably on the water's surface. Similarly, narrative writing without description added will rarely excite the reader. However, by adding description to narrative paragraphs, the writer will produce writing that is spirited and fun to read.

Reconsider the last example in which the soldier tells of his experiences in a rocket and mortar attack. This narration includes extensive use of description as the author attempts to help the reader visualize what occurred. In the second sentence, the writer could have continued his narrative by simply stating that "A movie was being shown." However, in order to be more graphic, the writer has written, "The rays of a movie projector danced in spasmodic beams of color through the foggy, moist air onto the deteriorated surface of an outdoor movie screen." Because of the elaborate visual description, the reader can more easily picture what the action was like when the mortar rounds began to fall nearby.

Descriptive writing is particularly effective in certain kinds of writing. *Report writing,* for instance, absolutely depends on good description. Without good description, an accident report will never be adequate. The difference can be monumental. A good example of the importance of description in narrative writing can be seen in the following examples. Both accounts narrate the same incident, but the second is far more useful because the description of the events is much more extensive.

### Accident Report

The accident occurred at 10:15 a.m. on March 23, 1976. Ten men were working with a crane and a front-end loader to lift and stack large concrete blocks when the crane's boom broke and fell across the front-end loader. The operator of the loader was struck by the boom as it fell. The boom was removed, and the operator taken to the hospital by ambulance.

### Accident Report

The accident occurred at 10:15 a.m. March 23, 1976, behind warehouse #154. Ten men were working with a crane and a front-end loader to lift and stack large concrete blocks which had been poured the previous day. Because the blocks had stuck to the concrete surface upon which they had been poured, the crane operator was experiencing serious difficulty lifting some of them. Consequently, the back of the crane would be lifted free of the surface each time the operator attempted to lift those which were stuck. After working for some time on those blocks that were seemingly stuck fast, a loud "crack" was heard from a point midway up the crane's boom. The boom swerved suddenly to the right and fell directly across the cockpit of the front-end loader with a loud crash. Unfortunately, the loader operator did not have time to escape from the cockpit before the boom struck. He did, however, have time to crouch down as low as possible before the boom hit him. When the weight of the 6,000 pound boom struck the operator, he was forced down into the cockpit with such violence that his face was jammed into the gear shift lever. Blood was everywhere in the cockpit and all of the men working on the same crew instantly assumed the operator had been killed by the crushing weight of the boom. The crew members immediately gathered together in a heroic but futile attempt to lift the boom off the man's shoulders; it was hopeless, however, and someone was dispatched to get a lift-truck which was used to raise the boom. Moments later the ambulance arrived, and the loader operator was carefully removed from the cockpit. Upon close inspection, the ambulance attendants determined that the man, although badly injured, was still alive, and they left for the hospital at top speed.

Here, good description works with narration to produce an account that is more interesting and far more detailed. For someone who did not view the accident, the first report, although accurate, fails to explain in enough depth to allow a clear picture of exactly what occurred.

But good descriptive writing does not need to be connected to a narrative. Occasionally, you will be asked to completely describe an object or person. The following paragraphs are **descriptive.** As you read them, notice that the authors have attempted to create word pictures of what they have seen: a hand, a man, a red-light district. They have explained what things look like and how they are arranged in relationship to one another. Notice that although the writers have communicated mainly what they have seen, they might also have included more details about what they felt, heard, or smelled. Nonetheless, these paragraphs illustrate the most important characteristic of descriptive writing: *a word picture of what it is that occupies a particular space.*

## 1

My hand is about average in size. I have long, slender fingers. There are four fingers and one thumb attached to my hand. All of my fingers have fingernails. My hand has all sorts of lines. On the back of my hand, there is some hair that I can hardly see. The hair also grows on the backs of my fingers and thumb. My fingers are very flexible. The bone joints are what make my hand and fingers flexible. Some of my joints have a little extra skin so I can bend them with ease. Each one of the joints in my fingers is about an inch apart from the others. When I lay my hand out flat on the table, the skin above my joints collapses so that there are little circles around the joint. The little circles have lines in them. When I make my hand into a fist, my skin tightens up, and the lines disappear. Also, when I make a fist I can see my veins on top of my joints. On the palm of my hand, I have lines running up and down and sideways. Some of the lines are short, and some are long. My hand is a flesh color with a little bit of pink in it. Around my fingers is a yellow color from smoking cigarettes all day. My fingernails are about the same color only a little more pink. My fingernails are a bit long, and the ends are white. On the bottom of my fingernails is a white half moon showing.

## 2

I first met Charley Crenshaw about three years ago while I was doing some first-hand research on the effects of cheap wine on the central nervous system. He was casually leaning against a soot-covered brick building, grinning at the rush-hour traffic. He wore an almost-black navy blue pea coat that had obviously at one time belonged to someone of twice Charley's stature. His dark green wool pants were almost as ill-fitting as his coat; indeed, they had apparently at one time in their long life been altered to fit a very short-legged man, which Charley was not. About five inches below these pants, Charley's ankles plunged into a pair of black, steel-toed work shoes. The bulbous toes of the work shoes gave Charley an unmistakable Bozo-the-Clown image of which I was sure he was very proud. To remember Charley's humorous blue eyes and his genuine laughter makes me recall the old cliche "You can't tell a book by its cover."

## 3

To imagine an avenue representative of all the pleasure streets of Europe is a formidable task indeed. But if one should decide to make this attempt, he should start with an old, narrow street lined with four-story buildings that make no effort at hiding the activities that take place in their neglected rooms. At the bottoms of these buildings are housed shops and taverns that are mutually conducive to the welfare of the street's purpose. While maybe half of these establishments are bars, randomly sprinkled along the way are shops specializing in the devices required for this kind of love. And intermingled with these reservoirs of libations and supermarkets of erotica, are the small lobbies with stairways of questionable safety leading to the many-roomed upper floors. But here is where the physical description must end, for this collection of brothels is only the setting for a scene that differs from mind to mind. Some, the ones in quest of pleasure, see only the new experiences to be had underneath the scant garb of buxom temptresses, while others, the wenches who have lived a million nights, see no further than the wallets of their aroused customers. So, to imagine this place of employment as old as man himself, one must concentrate on the emotions and experiences rather than attempt to draw his picture from the cracked walls and broken windows of the buildings themselves.

Now read a famous pair of poems by Robert Browning: *"Meeting at Night"* and *"Parting at Morning."* They contain some very fine descriptive lines. After considering the overall meaning of the poems, concentrate on the **description** conveyed in the individual lines. Their sensory appeal is multiple: the lines appeal to the reader's sense of sight, sense of hearing, sense of smell, and sense of touch. Furthermore, the description puts into perspective the relative arrangements of the sea, the land, and the sky. The readers get a picture of what lies at a distance and what is close at hand; they get a sense of motion, direction, and distance as they travel with the man who tells the story. The man, who should not be confused with the poet Robert Browning, is the speaker in both poems, but he describes some of the woman's actions: the man says that she lights a match, she speaks in fear and joy, and that her heart beats loudly. The first poem communicates the ecstatic joy of the two lovers, especially the man's, and the second poem seems to say, sadly but resolutely, that the raptures of romantic love are temporary and cannot last. The second poem seems to say that the joys of physical love are not sufficient. They do not endure, and, furthermore, the man is compelled to leave his love for more pressing tasks somewhere in the world of less romantic responsibilities. But note how finely tuned the narrator's senses are in the first poem. Under the influence of his heightened expectation, his perception is tremendous.

## MEETING AT NIGHT
### I

And the grey sea and the long black land;
And the yellow half-moon large and low;
And the startled little waves that leap
In fiery ringlets from their sleep,
As I gain the cove with pushing prow,
And quench its speed i' the slushy sand.

### II

Then a mile of warm sea-scented beach;
Three fields to cross till a farm appears;
A tap at the pane, the quick sharp scratch
And blue spurt of a lighted match,
And a voice less loud, thro' its joys and fears,
Than the two hearts beating each to each!

## PARTING AT MORNING

Round the cape of a sudden came the sea
And the sun looked over the mountain's rim:
And straight was a path of gold for him,
And the need of a world of men for me.

Write a paragraph that vividly *describes* a person, place, or thing.

_____

_____

_____

_____

_____

_____

_____

_____

_____

_____

_____

_____

_____

_____

_____

_____

_____

_____

_____

Now show your work to some of your classmates and to your instructor. Ask them if they think all of the lines are effective or how the description might be improved.

# LESSON THREE—Longer Narration and Description

**Narrative** and **descriptive** writing can be *combined* in papers longer than one paragraph very effectively. You must consider how you can use these kinds of writing in your life. Letter writing, of course, requires you to use both narration and description, but report writing also presents you with an opportunity to use both. Here are two examples that combine narration and description. Each was written by a student who was asked to narrate in detail a memorable event from the past.

## 1

In 1945, when I was nine years old, we were living in Gailoh, a small village in Bavaria, on the second floor of a very old farmhouse. My parents, my two brothers, and two sisters called two run-down rooms our home. We had just recently been evacuated from Bielitz, a medium-sized town in Silesia, Germany, now known as Bielsko, Poland, to escape the furies of World War II, and we children found life in this little country village fascinating and exciting. Approximately twenty farmhouses flocked around a tiny little chapel, situated in the middle of the village square. The roads, not paved, were dry and dusty in summer and dirty and muddy in winter. Next to the little chapel stood the shepherd's cottage. It resembled a sodhouse of the American Plains. The floor consisted of fine sand, and any time it needed cleaning, a new layer of sand was spread evenly over the last one. I marveled over this type of house, and to me the most beautiful sight was to see two hundred sheep bleating through the village, stirring up clouds of dust with their hooves. Life in Gailoh seemed so backward that I imagined myself transferred into the eighteenth century. My job was to pump drinking water into buckets and to carry them into the house. An outhouse per family was considered a luxury. We were the only Lutheran family among strict religious Roman Catholics.

During the month of May, all the villagers, young and old, would gather in the little chapel to pray the rosary; a priest would lead the prayers. "Ave Maria . . ." the congregation would chant over and over again, slipping beads through their fingers to keep count of each prayer. My friend Fanni, the shepherd's daughter, had to attend these evening services, and I would tag along, out of pure curiosity. It didn't make any sense to me to recite the same prayers over and over again, words swaying back and forth rhythmically like waves in the ocean.

One evening I decided to bring a little life and excitement into this hot and crowded church. I had spent all day catching great big brown May bugs in a huge cigar box. As usual, I went along with Fanni to church, but this time with the cigar box tucked under my arm. We entered the church, sprinkled a little water on our foreheads, and made the three crosses with the thumb of our right hands, murmuring: "In the name of the Father, the Son, and the Holy Ghost, Amen." I followed Fanni to the front pew, my heart pounding with anticipation. We knelt on the hard floor and recited Ave Maria, preceded by Pater Noster, and followed by Gloria Patri, over and over again. I had second thoughts about my brazen plan, but I decided to go through with it, especially since my brothers and sisters knew about it and expected some excitement. In the middle of the Pater Noster, I opened the lid of my cigar box and released a swarm of May bugs. It headed straight for the priest who was completely absorbed in his prayers. It circled his head, humming like a swarm of bees. I heard a giggle and then another, and soon all of the children in the chapel were giggling. The children had spotted this unbelievable phenomenon. Some May bugs flew against the windowpane with loud thuds. The whole congregation in the church started to stir: the prayers weren't clear and rhythmical any more. I was scared and ashamed of my deed.

Suddenly, I felt faint and very dizzy. The room started spinning like the May bugs around the priest's head. Everything turned black in front of my eyes. I groped my way out of the chapel, somehow. Half stumbling, half crawling along the dusty road, I made my way through the village, up the three steps to the first floor of the farmhouse. Then I called for my mother and fainted. When I woke up, I was lying on my bed, and my mother was bending over me with a concerned expression on her face. I felt like I was floating and drifting away. I was convinced that I was dying. Never had I experienced such a feeling before. "Dying isn't bad," I thought. According to my mother's report, I looked deathly sick. I was white as a sheet, and my lips were blue, drained of all their color.

The country doctor was called and diagnosed my condition as a severe case of anemia and malnutrition. I didn't agree with him. Secretly I was convinced that I was being punished for poor behavior in God's holy house.

## 2

As a result of never attending school, I was sent to juvenile hall where I learned a lesson that no school could provide. At this time in my life I looked up to people who tried to get something for nothing. I found a great number of these people in juvenile hall.

One of the most popular pastimes at the juvenile hall was formulating plans of escape. The inmates stood around in groups talking and planning. The leader of our particular group was a black man by the name of Al. Al, who was quite tall, had a massively strong build, and his face reflected a very hard life; however, contrary to his appearance, he was very well-adjusted. Al's almost religious attitude towards escape seemed to be the only flaw in his character. Although we participated in the discussions of escape, no one really seemed to take them seriously. Unfortunately, a new arrival eventually did. The new inmate's name was Joe. Joe also had a massive build. His presence made it apparent that he would not take guff from anyone. Joe's appearance and gruff personality made him a not very likeable person; nevertheless, we invited him into our group.

Al's most recent plan was quite simple. The escape was to take place in the recreation area. Someone was supposed to knock out the guard with a cuestick and take his keys, which, of course, were the keys to freedom. The only drawback to his plan was that there were no volunteers to knock out the guard—that is, no volunteers until Joe came along. Joe absorbed Al's every word. At the end of the discussion, Joe spoke without any hesitation. He said that he would "knock the guard's lights out."

It was the guard's first day on the job. Unwittingly, he was reading a book and was completely unaware of the different activities going on in the room. I was shooting pool as the most tragic experience I had ever encountered, or will probably ever encounter, was about to take place. Joe walked up and grabbed my opponent's cuestick. He clutched it as if he were holding a baseball bat by the small end. The guard looked up from his book just as Joe swung the stick with blinding speed. The shattering impact caved in the left side of the guard's head, and blood spurted out of his right ear. My mind screamed with terror. I was completely incoherent. A fellow inmate's fruitless efforts to stop Joe only resulted in him being knocked to the floor. Joe's second swing caved in the right side of the guard's head. As the cuestick smashed into his head, it made a sickening crunching sound that seemed to open up a reservoir of blood. Joe's third swing had more velocity than either of the first two. The guard was hit with such force that the cuestick broke in two about twelve inches from the top at the big end.

This final blow sent a lifeless form slowly falling to the floor. I felt like I was going to vomit. Joe and everyone else stood in complete disbelief, staring at the gory spectacle. The sight of the guard lying lifeless in the sickening pool of blood was incomprehensible. It was so horrible that no one would go near the guard to retrieve the keys. Then, suddenly, someone pushed the ALERT button. The guards were upon us instantly. They immediately rushed us off to our individual cells without making any effort to find out who the guilty party was. Then the guards rushed the badly injured guard off to the hospital. But their hurried efforts were needless. The guard was dead on arrival at the hospital.

Later, the guards began questioning the inmates one by one about the killing. When it came to my turn to be questioned, I replied that I had not seen or heard anything until after I was rushed off to my cell. Approximately ten minutes later, a guard opened my cell door. I was still sick to my stomach at the thought of the blood. When I was outside the door of my cell, the guard began shoving me around. He informed me that I would have to clean up the mess. The guard then handed me some towels. I started cleaning up the blood. I could not hold the sickness back any longer. I began vomiting all over the place.

About two days after the incident I was released from juvenile hall. I dreamed about the murder every night for about two weeks. Even now it occasionally haunts me. The whole thing had such an impact on me that I can still remember it vividly.

## EXERCISE 7

Write a paragraph or more in which you *combine description and narration.* You might write about an especially memorable experience of yours. Support your narration with accurate, specific descriptive details. As you write, try to remember everything you have learned in this unit.

Discuss your paragraph with an instructor.

# UNIT FOUR
## *The Thesis Sentence*

## *Objectives*

After completing this unit, you will be able to

1. select and limit a subject for writing a short composition.
2. define the terms *thesis sentence, topic sentence, controlling idea,* and *divided thesis*.
3. compose effective thesis sentences for short compositions.
4. divide thesis sentences into three parts.
5. identify the appropriate order of a *divided thesis*.
6. distinguish between a *thesis sentence* and a *topic sentence*.
7. create effective topic sentences.
8. locate topic sentences in sample paragraphs.
9. write thesis sentences and construct topic sentences for them.

# 4

Every composition you write must have a **beginning**, a **middle**, and an **end.** Moreover, each part must be effectively constructed, or the overall impression of your paper will suffer. The beginning portion of any composition will hereafter be referred to as the *introduction*, and it is the last sentence of the introduction, the *thesis* sentence, that is the most important sentence of the entire composition. Since you will not be asked to write a composition of more than one thousand words in *Writer's Workshop*, the thesis for your papers will only be one sentence in length.

Most of this unit is devoted to the effective construction of the thesis statement because the thesis is so important. Obviously, readers of your paper are going to read the introduction first, and their opinion of your total composition will begin to form as they read this beginning section. If your thesis is not well stated, if it does not clearly indicate what the paper is about, they may not read further. Since the thesis sentence is the high point of your introduction, it becomes apparent, then, that as it is with life, you must make the best first impression possible.

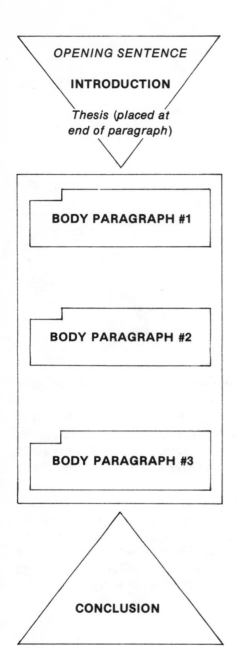

OPENING SENTENCE

INTRODUCTION

*Thesis (placed at end of paragraph)*

BODY PARAGRAPH #1

BODY PARAGRAPH #2

BODY PARAGRAPH #3

CONCLUSION

Before attempting to write a composition, you must be aware of the parts of it and how they fit together. The commonly assigned short paper might very well consist of the five paragraphs in the diagram at the left. The first paragraph is the **introduction**; its purpose is to prepare the reader for what is to be explained or argued in the body of the paper. It does this by narrowing from a broad **opening sentence** to a specific **thesis**—thus the triangle at the top of the diagram. Following the introduction are the body paragraphs. These paragraphs explain or support the thesis sentence (located at the end of the introductory paragraph). Finally, a concluding paragraph sums up the composition. The conclusion restates the thesis idea, then reviews the main evidence, and ends with a generalization—thus the triangle at the end of the diagram.

SPECIAL NOTE:

While a thesis sentence may be placed at any point in the introduction and while some compositions have only an implied thesis, you will be expected to write a one-sentence thesis for every introduction you write. In future writing courses you may wish to experiment with other techniques and arrangements, but first you must master this technique well. Improvizational jazz musicians first have to learn the basic melodies and patterns—only then can they develop new ones.

116

# LESSON ONE—Choosing a Subject

Many writers find the *selection of a good subject* to be one of the most difficult tasks of the whole writing process. While subject selection is very important and the necessary first step before you can write a thesis sentence, it certainly need not be the stumbling block that many students seem to feel it is. If you will follow a few simple steps and develop a logical, thoughtful procedure for choosing a good subject, your compositions will not only be much more interesting, but they will be easier to write.

### Ask Yourself Some Questions About the Assignment

Whenever you are faced with a writing assignment that requires you to choose your subject, answer the following essential questions about the assignment:

1. What are the *restrictions* on the assignment? May you write about anything you please, or is it necessary to confine your subject to some area such as history, science, sociology, or English? If you are restricted to the subject area of a particular class, may you write about anything related to that class or only on a subject your instructor assigned?

2. Within the stated restrictions, what are your *interests*? What do you already know about, or what do you wish to find out more about?

3. What is the *purpose* of the assignment? Are you to demonstrate that you know something particular about the subject, or are you to demonstrate that you can perform research in the subject area? Is it the form or the content that is of most importance in this assignment?

4. What is your *approach* to the subject? Should you simply demonstrate that you are generally knowledgable in the subject area, or should you try to convince a reader to subscribe to a particular point-of-view or that you have made a detailed study of some matter? Will it be necessary to write about broad aspects of your subject or only a part of it?

5. What is the *length* of the assignment? Are you to write a ten to twenty page research paper or a short 500-word composition?

Assume, for instance, that your sociology instructor has asked for a short paper (750-1000 words) on a current issue in contemporary American society. You know that marriage as an institution has undergone many controversial experiments and changes, and you are interested in exploring some of the questions that surround alternatives to marriage. The questions you asked above might be answered for your sociology paper on the subject of marriage as follows:

1. The *restriction* on the assignment is to write on the subject of the American family.

2. Your *interest* is in the future of the family as an institution in American life. Several of your friends are living together without marriage, and you would like to find out more about the possible importance of this trend.

3. The *purpose* of the assignment is to show that you can think and perform as a sociologist would and explore a sociological subject in some depth.

4. For this assignment, your *approach* will be to convince the reader of the logic and thoughtfulness of your point-of-view on a sociological trend.

5. In *length* the composition is not to be over one thousand words (four typed pages); therefore, it will be necessary to deal with only a small aspect of the subject. **117**

After answering the questions, you are ready to choose some tentative *topics* on the subject of marriage. At this point simply list ideas on your subject as they come to you. The following is one possible list:

1. The future of marriage as a viable institution in American life

2. The benefits of a trial marriage before the *real thing*
3. The moral implications of trial marriage
4. The most rapidly growing phenomena of heterosexual relationships: the arrangement—(living together)
5. Sexual relationships, children, and responsibilities for couples who live together without marriage
6. Liberating the couple to allow each partner to be equal within a lasting relationship.

You could go on and on listing possible topics for a subject such as this, but about five should be sufficient to give you some alternatives from which to choose. You should note, after writing your list of topics, that some are obviously too broad for a paper of no more than one thousand words in length. While they might work well for longer research papers of 2,000-3,000 words, such topics would be unmanageable for the short paper, so they should be either discarded or revised.

**EXERCISE 1**

You are now faced with a writing assignment that requires you to choose a **subject**. Pretend that you are in your favorite class and that your instructor has assigned the class a 1,000 word paper to be written on a subject of your choice, but it must be about the general subject matter under study in the class. Name the class and answer the following questions as you contemplate your composition subject.

Name of the class _____

1.What are the restrictions on the assignment?

_____

_____

_____

_____

2. What are your interests?

_____

_____

_____

_____

3. What is the purpose of the assignment?

_____

_____

_____

_____

4. What is your approach to the subject?

_____

_____

_____

_____

5. How long is the composition to be?

_____

_____

## EXERCISE 2

While you keep the answers to Exercise 1 in mind, choose three *subjects* about which you might like to write. (*Choose carefully*—do not make a selection unless the subject interests you because you will be asked to write several paragraphs on it. Your work will become tedious for you and your reader unless it interests you.)

Subject One  _____

_____

_____

Subject Two  _____

_____

_____

Subject Three  _____

_____

_____

To help determine which of the above subjects is the best for you, examine each of your three possibilities by asking the following questions about it:

1. Will the subject meet the requirements of the assignment?
2. Will the subject be appropriate for its intended readers?
3. Are you capable of writing on this subject?
4. Can the subject be easily limited so that you do not try to write too much for a short paper?
5. Can the subject be easily researched, if necessary?
6. Are you interested in the subject?
7. Can you honestly answer "yes" to the above six questions? If not, choose another subject, or justify your decision to continue with it.

Select one of the **subjects** you chose in Exercise 2, and write a short paragraph (four or five sentences) in which you explain why you chose the subject and why it is a good one.
one.

Subject: _____

_____

Explanation: _____

_____

_____

_____

_____

_____

_____

Have your work checked.

## LESSON TWO—Narrowing the Subject

Once you have chosen a general *subject*, you must consider ways to narrow it. The problem with most general subjects is that they are too broad in scope to develop into a short 500-1,000 word composition. One can hardly expect to deal effectively with a big subject such as crime, ecology, drugs, censorship, marriage, or abortion in a short paper without narrowing the subject. Without focus on a topic, the paper will simply be a weak review of some popular generalization; the paper will not have been worth the effort, as

120

your grade will illustrate. You can, however, avoid this pitfall simply by some thoughtful restrictions of the general subject.

## How Can the Subject Be Narrowed

After you have selected your subject, ask yourself some questions about it that will suggest ways you might narrow and restrict it so that it interests you:

A. Is there a *controversial aspect* of the subject that will allow you to write either for or against something? If so, can you limit your subject to one side of the controversy in such a way that you can write only about the advantages or the disadvantages of one particular point-of-view?

*Examples*

1. How censorship violates the First Amendment to the Constitution
2. The advantages of living together before marriage
3. Alcohol compared to marijuana

B. Is there a good way to narrow a broad subject by *restricting it to a particular time or place?*

*Examples*

1. The effects of Soviet censorship upon Russian artists during the 1960's
2. Switching sex roles between husbands and wives in Sweden
3. How the use of marijuana affects the study habits of students at State University

C. Is it possible to discuss some *historical aspect* of the subject?

*Examples*

1. Movie censorship during the 1920's
2. Marriage customs among the Hebrews during Christ's lifetime
3. The consequences of the use of alcohol upon the military personnel during World War II

D. Is there some way to limit the subject into some *natural divisions?*

*Examples*

1. Marriage: traditional, group, trial, common law, platonic
2. Censorship: military, press, pornography, political, school, books, movies, television, radio

E. Is there a way to *combine limitations* that will even further narrow the subject?

*Examples*

1. The effects of capital punishment upon crime in the South during the 1920's
2. Television censorship in American Samoa during the Nixon Administration
3. The role of sex in marriage for lower-caste couples in India

121

Many of these topic suggestions are still too broad for a short paper. Often these can be further restricted, but you should now be able to carry out some carefully considered subject narrowing on your own.

**EXERCISE 4**

For each of the general subjects below, list topics that you could develop into a composition of no more than 1,000 words.

A. Movies

1. _____

_____

_____

2. _____

_____

_____

3. _____

_____

_____

B. Money

1. _____

_____

_____

2. _____

_____

_____

3. _____

_____

_____

C. College

**122**

1. _____

_____

2. _____

_____

3. _____

_____

D. Love

1. _____

_____

2. _____

_____

3. _____

_____

_____

E. The subject you selected in Lesson One, Exercise 3, on page 120.

1. _____

_____

2. _____

_____

3. _____

_____

Have your work checked.

## LESSON THREE—Limiting the Topic

Once you have narrowed your general subject to some topics and selected one for development, you probably have what you need to begin to write a long paper. If, however, your assignment is to write a short paper—500-1,000 words—you will need to *limit your topic.*

**How can the topic be limited?**

After you have chosen a topic for a composition, consider what you wish to write about the topic. Usually you must limit yourself to two or three points, or the paper will become too long. You can reduce the scope of your paper by focusing on an aspect of your topic—that part of the topic that interests you enough to wish to write about it. For example, if you chose to write about the general subject of terrorism, you might have narrowed your subject as follows:

Subject—Terrorism

    TOPIC #1   Terrorism as a political technique

TOPIC #2   Terrorism's effect upon its surviving victims
TOPIC #3   The relationship between terrorism and religious fanaticism

*. . . limit yourself to two or three points.*

Once you have several topics, you may choose one for further limitation. Since Topic #2—Terrorism's effect upon its surviving victims—is still a broad topic, probably requiring several thousand words for full development, the topic must be limited in a way that will indicate just what you want to write about it. The topic limitation might proceed as follows:

Subject—Terrorism
    TOPIC #2   Terrorism's effect upon its surviving victims
        Limited topic #1   Victims' attitudinal change from fear, to sympathy, to love for terrorist captors
        Limited topic #2   Terrorist captors' attitude change from hate, to understanding, to sympathy for their victims
        Limited topic #3   Victims' physiological, sociological and psychological problems during captivity by terrorists

**EXERCISE 5**

Limit each of the topics listed below.

A. The disadvantages of living together before marriage

**124**   Limited topic: _____

_____

_____

_____

B. Switching sex roles between husbands and wives

Limited topic: _____

_____

_____

_____

C. The consequences of alcohol abuse by teenagers

Limited topic: _____

_____

_____

_____

D. Limit the topic you chose for Section E of Exercise 4 for Lesson Two on page 123.

Your topic: _____

_____

Your limited topic: _____

_____

_____

_____

_____

_____

Have your work checked.

# LESSON FOUR—The Thesis Statement

After you have narrowed your subject to a topic and limited the topic so that it may be developed into a short composition, you are ready to write your **thesis statement**. The most important single sentence in your whole paper, the thesis, tells the reader just what your composition is all about. If the composition is argumentative, the thesis tells readers what it is you are trying to persuade them to believe; if it is an informative paper, it tells them, without elaboration, your main idea or ideas.

While the thesis statements of long compositions may be two or three sentences in length, the thesis for a short paper—the type you will write in this book—should not be more than *one* sentence (thus you will hear many people speak of the thesis *sentence* rather than the *thesis statement*). Since the thesis is so important, it must be written skillfully and thoughtfully, and if you approach its writing logically, the thesis is not at all difficult.

You will be most successful in writing thesis statements if you have been careful to follow the series of simple steps as you limited your topic. Suppose, for example, that you are instructed to write a short composition on the subject of animal behavior in your psychology class. To avoid ruining your composition by writing a poor thesis sentence, proceed step-by-step to narrow your subject to a carefully written topic that then may be limited in a way that summarizes exactly what you want to write in the rest of your paper; then write your thesis.

*The Steps:*

1. Decide upon your **subject**. (This is often determined by your assignment.)
   —Animal Behavior

2. Narrow your subject to several possible writing **topics** that deal with the subject of animal behavior.
   —The porpoise off the Pacific Coast
   —The gooney birds of the Midway Islands
   —The alligators of southern swamps
   —Bears in national parks

3. Select one of the topics, and **limit it** so that it can be developed into a short paper.
   —The gooney birds of the Midway Islands
   —The mating dance of the gooneys
   —The humorous antics of gooneys taking off and landing
   —The war between the gooneys and the U.S. Navy

4. Transform the limited topic chosen into several versions of thesis sentences that may be effective.
   —The continuing conflict between the United States Navy and the gooney birds of Midway Island illustrates the strength of the birds' determination to remain on the island of their birth.
   —In spite of the United States Navy's drive to rid Midway Island of gooney birds, the birds seem determined to remain on the islands where they were born.

—The gooney birds of Midway Island, even after several attempts by the United States Navy to drive them away, seem as determined as ever to remain on the island of their birth.

After considering the three thesis sentences above, suppose you choose to develop the first statement—the continuing conflict between the United States Navy and the gooney birds of Midway Island illustrating the strength of the birds' determination to remain on the island of their birth. If you did not already know enough about the birds, you would, of course, have to begin by doing some reading on the subject. After you had acquired sufficient information, you could begin your paper by developing your thesis statement. Since the composition will be short, a one-sentence thesis should be sufficient; nevertheless, it must reflect exactly what you want to write without being too simple. For instance, a statement such as *"I am going to tell you about the gooney birds"* would never do because it not only sounds like an opening line in a journal, but it is not interesting and is too broad for a short paper.

The thesis statement places absolute restrictions on the scope of a composition. For example, you could write several volumes on the subject of animal behavior. If you want to write a book on that subject, you would *not* need to narrow it to a topic of gooney birds, as in Step Two. Even some limited versions of the topic could easily be developed into a twenty to thirty-page paper; therefore, it is especially important to narrow your thesis sentence adequately. It is clear from the thesis above that the intention is to illustrate only the point about the birds' determination. Thus, both writer and reader know exactly what is to be discussed and the paper's direction after the thesis.

The gooney bird thesis chosen above restricts the author to a discussion of only some of the Navy's attempts to drive the gooneys away, and nothing else. Anything else would be irrelevant and would be considered a serious writing flaw. Consequently, once the selection of the conflict between gooneys and Navy has been made, the writer must omit anything about mating behavior or humorous antics, no matter how interesting they may be—those are topics for another composition.

By following the steps used in developing the gooney bird thesis, you should now be able to write a thesis sentence that will keep your paper directly on the topic. By continuously checking back to your thesis sentence, you will prevent your paper from wandering into irrelevant ideas. Checking back also helps you make certain that you discussed everything that you indicated in your thesis. You want to cover everything you promised your reader and no more.

## EXERCISE 6

Following the steps below, develop a thesis for the general subject *Crime*.

Step One—*Subject*: crime

Step Two—*Potential Topics:*
1. influence of television
2. victimless crimes
3. capital punishment
4. white collar crimes
5. prison reform

Step Three—Select a topic and limit it.

Topic: (Choose one from the above list.) _____

Limited Topic: _____

_____

_____

Step Four—The Thesis Statement: (Write a thesis sentence for a short composition of 500-1,000 words.)

_____

_____

_____

## EXERCISE 7

After copying your *subject, topic,* and *limited topic choice* from Lessons One, Two, and Three, create a **thesis sentence**. Write with care as you may write a composition from this thesis later in this book.

Step One—*Subject:* (Write the subject you chose to limit in Exercise 3 of Lesson One on page 120.)

_____

_____

_____

Step Two—*Topic*: (Write one of the general topics you chose for Section E of Exercise 4 for Lesson Two on page 123.)

_____

_____

_____

Step Three—*Limited Topic*: (Write the limited topic you chose for Section D of Exercise 5 for Lesson Three on page 125.)

_____

**128** _____

_____

Step Four—*Thesis Sentence:* (Write two versions of a thesis sentence for a 750-word composition from the limited topic you wrote in Step Three above.)

Version #1 _____

_____

_____

_____

_____

_____

Version #2 _____

_____

_____

_____

_____

Have your work checked.


# LESSON FIVE—The Divided Thesis

One of the most important steps in developing a thesis for a short composition is to decide exactly what is your main idea or argumentative position. This you must write out carefully and thoughtfully, including whatever controlling devices are needed to assure that your reader will know exactly what the entire paper will attempt to communicate.

One good method of controlling your composition is to *divide* your thesis into two or three parts. The *complex sentence* is generally the most effective for a divided thesis because it indicates to the reader just what your most significant point is by placing it in the *independent clause*. Your reasons for making this point or any qualifications of your point that need to be stated can be summarized in the *dependent clause*. This dependent clause shows that your reasons or qualifications are subordinate to or less important than your main point. At other times you may wish to show that your reasons or qualifications are important, so they should be emphasized by placement in the independent clause. The dependent clause for such complex sentences should contain ideas that are important to the full understanding of your point but not as important as the main idea. If your thesis sentence is well divided, your paper will naturally divide into sections that make the whole composition easier for you to write and more logical and readable for your reader.

**129**

The examples below illustrate how thesis sentences can be *divided* to more effectively control the whole composition and more precisely indicate to the reader what is to be discussed. In each instance the undivided thesis is satisfactory for a long paper; however, for a short composition the divided thesis is more effective.

(Undivided)  Sailboat racing is a demanding sport.
(Divided)    If sailors possess *skill, endurance,* and *determination,* they can win at sailboat racing.

The three qualifications—the conditions under which sailors can win—are listed in the dependent clause. The main idea—that sailors can win—is emphasized by its placement in the independent clause.

(Divided)    Sailboat racing requires *skill, endurance,* and *determination* if one expects to win.

Here, the conditions under which sailors can win are limited in the independent clause; consequently, the winning is subordinated to the condition.

(Undivided)  The novel *Cane* seems very contemporary
(Divided)    Because the author uses effective *imagery, characterizations,* and *setting,* the novel *Cane* seems contemporary although it was written in 1923.

Here, the reasons for *Cane's* timeless appeal are subordinated to the fact that the novel seems contemporary.

(Divided)    Although the book was written in 1923, the author's use of *imagery, characterizations,* and *setting* make *Cane* seem contemporary.

In this version the reasons for *Cane's* contemporary appeal are emphasized in the independent clause.

(Undivided)  Pollution is too broad a subject for an effective paper.
(Divided)    Although pollution is of national concern, the subject is too broad if students want their papers to be *well-written* and *persuasive.*
(Divided)    A *well-written* and *persuasive* composition on the subject of pollution will be far too broad if one wants to communicate effectively.

By dividing your thesis you not only let your reader know just what to expect, but you make it easier to stick to the point. Note how the complex sentence lends itself readily to division because the reader can immediately determine a composition's purpose and emphasis. In the divided theses on *Cane* (above), for example, you can readily see that the writer is helped to stick to the point by the limits placed upon the paper. Any discussion of anything but "imagery, characterizations, and setting" would be absolutely irrelevant.

**130**

**EXERCISE 8**

The following undivided thesis sentences may be made more effective by narrowing through *division.* Divide each one in such a way that the composition would obviously be limited, writing a *complex sentence* for each.

1. Skin diving can be dangerous.

_____

_____

2. The energy crisis is posing some serious problems.

_____

_____

3. A law should be passed to prevent pollution.

_____

_____

4. Censorship is harmful to a democracy.

_____

_____

5. (Divide one of the thesis sentences you wrote for Step Four in Exercise 7 of Lesson Four on page 128 and 129.)

_____

_____

Have your work checked.


## The Order of Division

As you *divide* your thesis, you should be considering in what *order* to place the divisions. The divided parts must be ordered logically, or your reader might become confused. For instance, if you describe how something has changed with time, start from the earliest time and *work toward the most recent.*

> A comparison of the nudity in movies of the 1940's with that in the movies of the 1970's suggests that Americans might yet overcome their Puritanical sexual inhibition.

*or*

> Because at birth they are so dependent on their mothers, at mating they are so vulnerable, and at death they are so useful, whales are an endangered species.

*or*

> Because the 1964 tidal wave started in Alaska, killed twelve people in Crescent City, California, and alarmed islanders as far away as Samoa, a tidal wave early warning system should be established.

*Time order* is not always useful; therefore, other kinds of divisions need to be considered. When location is involved, for example, your emphasis is usually most readily understood by your reader if you begin with the most distant part of your subject and *progress to the nearest.*

> Political apathy must be reversed on the federal, state, and local level if America is to remain a democracy.

> *or*

> The average American is becoming progressively less satisfied with his situation as federal, state, and local taxes increase faster than wages.

When dividing, be particularly careful to make your point strongly. In the first example above, the thesis statement would be far weaker if it simply read, "Political apathy must be reversed on the federal, state, and local level." Without the rest of the sentence, the reader would never know why political apathy must be reversed.

Another commonly used technique of ordering is by *importance.* When you present your discussion in your composition, you should save your *most important* supporting material for the *last.* If you present your best arguments first, the remainder of the paper will seem progressively less and less important to the reader. When properly written, the thesis sustains the reader's attention until the very last. Written this way, then, your thesis becomes an outline to be followed as you develop your paper. Consider the following thesis:

> Research into creating new life forms should be delayed because it is too expensive and because it may endanger the health and safety of humans.

Whenever you divide your thesis sentence into parts, you must be certain the body of your composition develops those parts in exactly the same order you listed them in your thesis. In the example above, the endangering of the "health and safety of humans" is far more important than the expense of the research; therefore, you should save the explanation of the health and safety hazard until after you have discussed the research's expense.

## EXERCISE 9

In the blank before each of the following thesis sentences, write *time, location,* or *importance* to identify the ordering technique used to divide each. (Answers on page 144)

_____ 1. Freeways are a good investment for the motorist because they save time, nerves, and lives.

_____ 2. Air pollution must be stopped since it causes discolored skies, damage to buildings, and lung cancer.

_____ 3. If people want to maintain their good health, they must have a nutritious breakfast, a light, wholesome lunch, and a well-balanced dinner.

_____ 4. Welfare reform has become a political issue in Washington, D.C., in California, and in San Francisco because of the ever-increasing number of people receiving welfare assistance.

_____ 5. Whales should be protected because they are such awesome creatures to behold and because they are so important to the ecology of the oceans.

132

_____ 6. Many people think that if a relationship progresses slowly from first date to engagement and swiftly from engagement to marriage the union will be more likely to last.

_____ 7. Because Australia, Tahiti, and Hawaii are the best sources of spare parts, the cruising sailor should plan to put into each when following the trade winds across the Pacific.

_____ 8. J.M. Synge's play *Deidre* has never been a success on stage because it was written in dialect and because the author died before he completed it.

## EXERCISE 10

In the blank after each of the following thesis sentences, rewrite any thesis sentence that is incorrectly *ordered*. Write *C* in the blank after any correctly ordered sentence. (Answers on page 144)

1. The oil spill caused by the collision of the freighters was a disaster because it killed thousands of birds and fish, stained the paint on pleasure boats, and discolored rocks on the shoreline.

_____

_____

2. The United States has military bases at home, in Europe, and in England because the threat of aggression still exists.

_____

_____

3. For dinner last night we had steak and potatoes, a cocktail, and cheesecake.

_____

_____

4. The year 1976 was interesting because that was the year the movie about the South, *Gone With the Wind,* was first presented on television and because a Southerner, Jimmy Carter, was elected President of the United States.

_____

_____

5. For the Marines, the invasion of Guam meant storming the beach, riding in small boats in a rough ocean, and digging foxholes in the sand.

_____

_____

## LESSON SIX—The Topic Sentence

**What Is a Paragraph?**

A **paragraph** is a related group of statements that is set off at the beginning by *indention*. A paragraph may stand by itself, but usually paragraphs are components in a larger composition. As you know, sentences develop their fullest meaning only when they are organized into a series of closely related statements. When groups of sentences are all about the same idea—for example, when they explain, illustrate, analyze, or argue the idea, they become a paragraph. However, when the writer wants to develop another idea, even if it is related to the first one, he must begin a new paragraph.

Paragraphs, in turn, are parts, or subdivisions, of a larger work—a composition. They are, however, completed thought developments that may stand alone. Each composition is composed of three types of paragraphs: **introductory**, **body**, and **concluding**. A short paper usually has only one introductory paragraph and only one concluding paragraph. It does, however, have several body paragraphs, each of which develops some part of the thesis statement. Nothing may be introduced into any paragraph that does not elaborate upon something suggested in the thesis; therefore, a well-written, thoughtful thesis should keep the body paragraphs on the subject.

**The Topic Sentence**

In the following example from a long paper, notice how the paragraph stands alone, a complete idea. Observe how it is held together by the *first sentence*, even though it is but a part of a whole composition.

**134**

> *Some photographs have such remarkable impact that they have the power to disturb people for days after they view them.* The visual documentation of the gruesome aspects of war or the degenerative effects of aging, for example, have only recently been included in photographic exhibits and books. A book like *Gramp*, which chronicles the last three years of life of a man in his eighties, is not pleasant viewing, but it is of great social importance because most people need a greater understanding of the natural processes of aging. One memorable photo,

for instance, shows Gramp's four-year-old great-granddaughter holding his hand the day of his death. People often forget that there need be no line between art and social conscience. The photographs with the most power to disturb people merge art and social conscience for their impact.

As is the case with the above example, one sentence in any body paragraph is far more important than any of the other sentences. This important sentence is the one that contains the main thought: the thought that each subsequent sentence either develops further or illustrates.

Put another way, this important sentence contains the *central point of the whole paragraph.* It explains what the paragraph is all about, what the topic of the paragraph is; consequently, it is called the **topic sentence**. Actually, a topic sentence states the overall idea of the paragraph as the thesis sentence does for the whole composition. The topic sentence may, in turn, be followed by supporting sentences showing smaller divisions within the paragraph. (These smaller divisions of support sentences will be discussed in the next unit.) The thesis sentence, then, states the writer's position on a subject for a composition while a topic sentence indicates the main idea to be developed in a paragraph. The thesis sentence holds the whole composition together; topic sentences control the individual body paragraphs.

### Do Not Confuse Thesis and Topic Sentences

Since the previous lesson dealt with the thesis sentence, and this lesson is, by contrast, concerned with the topic sentence, you should take especial note of the differences between the two. The two kinds of sentences are not alike. *Thesis sentences are found **only** in introductory paragraphs; topic sentences are found **only** in body paragraphs.* Turn back to the introduction to this unit. Review the outline, and observe the locations of the thesis sentence and the topic sentences.

Because the topic sentence contains the central idea of the paragraph, it will frequently be the most abstract or general sentence in it, though it should not be pointlessly broad. Read the following topic sentences, noting that they contain the topic as well as a comment on the topic.

1. Since they are often idealized and unrealistic, the principles of a nation are not revealed in its advertisements.
2. A generation ago people taught their children to be responsible for each other, to take care of one another, to share more with one another.
3. Until this year, George despised America for what he considered its bigotry, sterility, and "uptightness."
4. Many people still profess to believe in God and the Bible, but many of them seem not to understand the meaning of religion.
5. Unlike other comic book heroes, Marvel's heroes resembled real people.

### Focus Your Topic Sentence

You must be careful not to write topic sentences that are *too broad,* for they will lack focus. This lack of focus invites sweeping generalizations and unproven examples in the paragraph. Topic sentences that are so excessively broad lack direction; they give no indication of the author's intentions. For example:

### Too Broad

*Zen and the Art of Motorcycle Maintenance,* by Robert M. Pirsig, is an interesting book.

### Better

*Zen and the Art of Motorcycle Maintenance*, by Robert M. Pirsig, is a fascinating inquiry into American values.

### Too Broad

College students are not the same as they used to be.

### Better

College students are much older and more experienced now than they were during the 1950's.

What each of the "better" examples contains is a comment on the topic or a **controlling idea.** The controlling idea *limits* the scope of the topic sentence. It is important to limit the topic sentence in order to keep the paragraph from rambling on and on without any apparent direction. "Censorship has gone too far" is too broad for one paragraph. One might be able to write a reasonable paragraph on this subject if it contained a controlling idea: for example, "Censorship went too far last week when five books were removed from the library." Also, one must keep in mind that the topic sentence must cover all of the ideas or examples in the paragraph. The controlling idea, therefore, must be narrow enough to be the subject of a paragraph of reasonable length but not so narrow that any sentence in it could be outside the scope of the topic sentence.

Revise each of the following topic sentences by including a *controlling idea* that will give it a focus and direction.

1. City life is not all bad.

 

 

2. Television programs are a waste of time.

 

 

3. A college education is important.

 

 

4. Art is necessary to one's life.

 

 

Have your work checked.

## The Thesis Statement and the Topic Sentence Are Related

Looking at the topic sentence another way, it is a generalization or a general statement of an idea stated or implied in the thesis sentence. In other words, the topic sentence elaborates upon some part of the thesis. By generalizing in topic sentences, writers can concisely preview their ideas and opinions at the beginning of paragraphs. Then in subsequent sentences, those that follow the topic sentence can either elaborate or illustrate the general ideas expressed in the topic sentences. In the following example, note how the topic sentences relate to the thesis sentence.

*Example—*

*Thesis Sentence:*  Although it appears easy, successful sailing requires alertness, knowledge, and responsibility.

*Topic Sentence:*  1. The winds blowing upon a sailboat may shift, increase, or drop at a moment's notice; consequently, the sailor must be able to respond quickly.

*Topic Sentence:*  2. In addition to the wind, wave action can greatly affect a sailboat's progress through the water, so the sailor must know the sea well.

*Topic Sentence:*  3. Further, the sailor is responsible for the safety of his boat, his crew, and others upon the water.

**137**

Write a *thesis sentence* with **three** *topic sentences* following each. Avoid needless abstractions.

1. (Movies) Thesis Sentence:

_____

_____

_____

_____

   I. Topic Sentence:

_____

_____

_____

_____

   II. Topic Sentence:

_____

_____

_____

_____

   III. Topic Sentence:

_____

_____

_____

_____

**138**  2. (A current social problem) Thesis Sentence:

_____

_____

_____

_____

I. Topic Sentence:

_____

_____

_____

II. Topic Sentence:

_____

_____

_____

III. Topic Sentence:

_____

_____

_____

_____

3. Write the thesis statement you wrote for Step 5 of Exercise 8 in Lesson Five on page 131 and write a topic sentence for each division in the thesis.

Your Thesis Sentence:

_____

_____

_____

_____

I. Topic Sentence:

_____

_____

_____

_____

II. Topic Sentence:

_____

_____

_____

_____

III. Topic Sentence:

_____

_____

_____

_____

Have your work checked.


## BEGIN WITH THE TOPIC SENTENCE

Another point to remember, not only in writing but also as an aid to more effective reading, is that the topic sentence, the generalization, is frequently *the first sentence* in the body paragraph. Almost all textbook paragraphs begin with topic sentences. As a general rule, try to make the first sentence in each of your body paragraphs the topic sentence. As a result, your compositions will be easy to read.

*Example—*

*The supersonic transport's (SST) technological problems, still unsolved, were reason enough not to produce such an airplane.* For instance, the SST would have travelled at a speed faster than sound and in the stratosphere at an altitude of 65,000 feet. The air turbulence at this altitude, caused by colliding rivers of cold and warm air, would be far greater than at a lower level. These winds could toss a plane like "a rat shaken by a dog," causing many passengers to become airsick easily. Pilots had hoped to be able to detect these winds with infrared heat-detection devices that were being developed, but when a pilot is covering a mile every two seconds, the infrared detectors would have to be able to give a 150-mile advance warning. Engineers have not yet found a solution to this problem.

**140**

Although paragraphs with the topic sentences first are by far the most common and probably the easiest to write, the topic sentence may be placed within or at the end of the paragraph. *Although you will not use this technique in this book*, you should know that by placing the topic sentence within the paragraph or at the end, the writer can lead readers to the main idea rather than confronting them with it at the first.

*Example—*

The far-off strains of band music can be heard with each new gust of wind. An island of mysterious caves and tunnels becomes a haven for runaways and fugitives from parental justice. Not far away, a minstrel show is in progress on a flower-bedecked verandah of a New Orleans home. The screams of jungle animals over a fresh kill mingle with the tinkling music of the Swiss Alps. *Disneyland, designed for children, has become every adult's fantasy as well*. It is sometimes quite difficult to explain the fascination the park has for people, especially parents. Turn an adult loose among Mickey Mouse, the Pirates of the Caribbean, and the Matterhorn and bingo!!! Suddenly he is sporting mouse ears or a *genuine* Davy Crockett coonskin cap, and in this reverse situation, Junior is often embarrassed by his parent's inexplicable antics. Little does he realize, however, that his sire has merely reverted, and it will only be a short time before the family returns to the motel where Daddy can be tucked into bed, clutching his Dumbo the Elephant and dreaming of dancing Tahitian beauties.

## EXERCISE 13

Circle the letter before the *topic sentence* in each of the following paragraphs. (Answers on page 144.)

1. (A) Efforts to revise or abolish the electoral college system of voting for the President have occurred for nearly two hundred years. (B) More than five hundred proposals and bills to amend the Constitution have been made since 1787. (C) Some of the proposals would divide the nation into small electoral districts that would vote separately for the President. (D) Others would divide each state's electoral vote proportionately in the hope of at least approximating the popular will. (E) Only one solution has ever been made, however, that would assure that the person who most Americans wanted would be the President: a direct popular vote of the people with no institutional obstacle between the people and their chief executive.

2. (A) One can make smug little plans for future-itineraries for the "sights" of Europe, applications for jobs and "positions," plans for a career that is pure selfishness and which, called by any other name, would stink just as much of hedonism. (B) In India, a country filled with hungry, hollow-eyed people, it is quite impossible to be complacent and not to realize just how

**141**

fortunate it is to be an American. (C) By contrast, Americans seem to have it all: freedom of mobility, opportunity, and money. (D) The irony is that even when confronted with the ludicrous and awful, most feel no shame. (E) Rather, they take everything as if it were rightfully theirs, as if somehow it is deserved more for them than the majority of the world's population that never eats enough, that dies with mucous crusts on their eyeballs and knots of worms in their bellies.

3. (A) Recently, considerable criticism has been leveled against the schools and colleges of America for not adequately developing the writing skills of students. (B) The critics complain that all too many graduates of the public school system cannot write acceptable compositions for college entrance, and further, that students write little better upon completing college. (C) The evidence is preponderantly on the side of those who are demanding more value for their education and tax money. (D) Nearly two-thirds of all incoming college freshmen fail to qualify for the standard college composition course. (E) Furthermore, those who graduate from college increasingly demonstrate their lack of training in writing when required to write in their new jobs. (F) Clearly, educators must give more attention to what the critics are saying about writing skills in America.

4. (A) Those people who do not believe in God are often honest, independent, and trusting individuals who have a feeling of confidence and understanding of themselves and others. (B) Not believing in the God-myth tends to let people be more honest with themselves and others. (C) These people do not need God to build up their confidence because they rely on themselves. (D) From the self-trust they project, they soon find trust in others, who in turn find it easy to trust in them. (E) These people do not have any emptiness in their lives from their lack of religion, but rather they are much more full-of-life because of it.

5. (A) In January, 1968, the world's mightiest navy ignored the desperate pleas for assistance from a ship about to be captured. (B) Unknown to the commander of this ship, highly classified documents were aboard his vessel, a vessel supposedly conducting oceanic research. (C) For the next several months, two nations bombarded each other with accusations and diatribes while eighty-two men were brutalized behind prison walls, subjected to cruel and inhuman punishment, and treated like animals. (D) Their release was only secured when the more powerful of the two countries bowed to the demands of the lesser and signed an apology nearly a year later. (E) The subsequent court-martial of the commander of the ship was conducted for the violation of the famed "Military Code of Conduct." (F) One of the prosecution's arguments was that the commander, who was responsible for saving the lives of his crew, should not have surrendered his ship. (G) In the course of the proceedings, the defense revealed that vital information regarding the ship's mission was passed from bureau to bureau in the Department of

Navy and never reached those responsible. (H) By the end of the trial, however, the Navy succeeded in "passing the buck" from the highest echelons down to one man. (I) The "Pueblo Incident" will go down in history as yet another outrageous example of the cold insensibility of the government and the ranking military regime for the ordinary fighting man.

# Answers for Unit Four Exercises

The following are suggested answers for the exercises on the preceding pages. If your answers do **not** agree with the suggested answers on this page, have your work checked.

**Exercise 9 (page 132)**

1. importance
2. importance
3. time
4. location
5. importance
6. time
7. location
8. importance

**Exercise 10 (page 133)**

1, The oil spill caused by the collision of the freighters was a disaster because it stained the paint on pleasure boats, discolored rocks on the shoreline, and killed thousands of birds and fish.
2. The United States has military bases in Europe, in England, and at home because the threat of aggression still exists.
3. For dinner last night we had a cocktail, steak and potatoes, and cheesecake.
4. *C*
5. For the Marines, the invasion of Guam meant riding in small boats in a rough ocean, storming the beach, and digging foxholes in the sand.

**Exercise 13 (page 141)**

1. A
2. B
3. A
4. A
5. I

# UNIT FIVE

## *Developing Body Paragraphs— Basic Considerations*

## *Objectives*

After completing this unit, you will be able to

1. evaluate the effectiveness of *topic sentences.*
2. identify and write *topic sentences, primary support sentences, secondary support sentences,* and *concluding sentences* in body paragraphs.
3. understand the concept of *support clusters.*
4. expand or reduce body paragraphs that are too long or too short.
5. use *explanations, examples, facts* and *statistics, quotations,* and *anecdotes* that provide specific support for generalizations.
6. revise sentences that are *too general* or *too obvious.*
7. rewrite a body paragraph so that the sentences in it *connect smoothly.*
8. write a *well-developed body paragraph.*

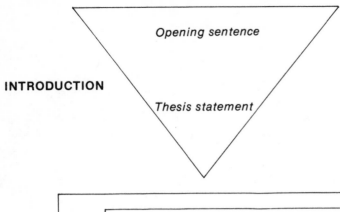

**INTRODUCTION**

*Opening sentence*

*Thesis statement*

In your opening sentence introduce the subject and capture your reader's attention; then the paragraph should gradually narrow to a very specific thesis sentence.

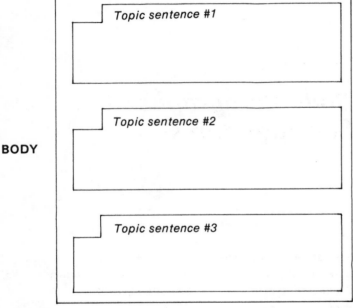

**BODY**

*Topic sentence #1*

*Topic sentence #2*

*Topic sentence #3*

In the body of your paper present whatever is required to support the assertion your thesis makes.

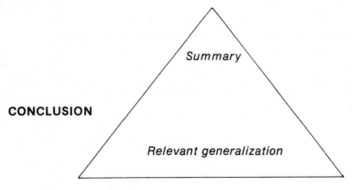

**CONCLUSION**

*Summary*

*Relevant generalization*

The concluding paragraph, in direct contrast to your introductory paragraph, should begin with the specific point and broaden to a general or universal application of your point.

**146**    Once you have developed a thesis statement and its accompanying topic sentences, you have accomplished the most difficult part of a paper's development. The remainder of the process is relatively easy. However, before you get to the business of this unit—*writing body paragraphs*—you must be certain that you thoroughly understand the diagram that is shown above. For the present time, you will not concern yourself with the development of the introductory paragraph. Rather, you will begin with the body paragraphs because they make up the portion of the paper which communicates your message. When these paragraphs are deliberately developed according to an accepted procedure, you will find them not difficult to write.

# 5

## LESSON ONE—More Practice With Topic Sentences

Your reader should be able to read the first sentence of any one of the **body paragraphs** in your composition and understand immediately where the paragraph is heading. As you learned in Unit Four, every body paragraph must be *clearly focused*, and the best way to give each one that direction is to build it around a strong **topic sentence**. Briefly, the following are the qualities of an effective topic sentence:

—A clearly stated topic sentence tells the reader the *main point* of the paragraph.

—Every topic sentence should be *sufficiently limited*.

—The *controlling idea* of the topic sentence should be plainly stated.

### EXERCISE 1

Circle the number of the *best* topic sentence. In evaluating the sentences, use the following criteria: main point evident, topic sufficiently limited for a five-to-ten sentence paragraph, controlling idea plainly stated. (Answers on page 165)

1. The purpose of this paragraph is to cover the reasons against building the dam.
2. Some people are for the dam, and some people are against it.
3. The dam should not be built.
4. The federal government must not allow unrestricted cutting of forests, unsafe dams, or new factories that pollute the atmosphere.
5. The curved-arch design of the Granite Gorge dam is not safe.

**147**

A good topic sentence also tells the reader *how the body paragraph fits into the framework of the entire composition.*

—The topic sentence must be written so that the relationship of the topic sentence to the composition's thesis is easily seen.

—Whenever possible, the topic sentence should be placed at the *very beginning of the body paragraph*—the first sentence of the paragraph.

—The topic sentence may function as a *transitional sentence* because it helps the reader connect other paragraphs in the composition.

**EXERCISE 2**

Circle the numbers of the *two* thesis-topic sentence combinations that seem *best* in terms of the following criteria: obvious relationship between topic sentences and thesis, topic sentences suitable for opening sentences of body paragraphs, topic sentences helpful as transitional sentences. (Answers on page 165)

1. *Thesis*: Winston's rebellion in Orwell's *1984* takes place in stages.
   *Topic Sentences:*
   Winston's first act of rebellion is to purchase a forbidden diary.
   Winston's second act of rebellion is to engage in a secret affair with Julia.

2. *Thesis:* Some science-fiction fanatics objected to the movie *Star Wars* as being too unrealistic.
   *Topic Sentences:*
   For example, the critics thought the creatures in the spaceport saloon were too unbelievable.
   George Lucas, who wrote and produced the film, insisted on calling the movie a "space fantasy."

3. *Thesis:* The single-family dwelling may be too expensive for most Americans by the turn of the century.
   *Topic Sentences:*
   The median cost of a new home is already more than $50,000.
   By the turn of the century the average home will probably cost more than $200,000.

## LESSON TWO—Developing Body Paragraphs

Once you have stated your topic sentence at the beginning of a body paragraph, you must add sentences that *develop* the controlling idea of the topic sentence. You must further *explain* or *argue* the primary idea or the separate points introduced in the topic sentence. This discussion must be thorough enough and detailed enough that every reader will understand what you are saying.

PRIMARY AND SECONDARY SUPPORT SENTENCES

**Primary Support Sentences**

**148**

A **primary support sentence** is any sentence in a body paragraph that directly elaborates upon the controlling idea of the topic sentence. A primary support sentence may restate, explain, break down, add to, illustrate, or argue in support of what is said in the topic sentence. A body paragraph may have just one primary sentence or several, depending on how many are needed.

The topic sentence plus the primary sentences form the *framework*, or skeleton, of

*You must explain . . . the separate points introduced.*

the paragraph. These sentences *outline* the paragraph, and by reading the topic and primary support sentences alone, a reader can understand the paragraph's general meaning.

*Examples*

**1**

**TS** *Marvel comics were more interesting and realistic because of the constant change they all exhibited.* **PS** For example, the character relationships were not static.

**2**

**TS** *Debbie finds the men who frequent the school cafeteria boring because, to her, almost all of those men fit too easily into one of three stereotyped groups.* **PS** The Blacks sit together at a double row of tables by the front doors. **PS** A second group, the veterans, sit at a long row of tables near the cash registers. **PS** A third group, the cowboys, all lean their chairs against the west wall.

**3**

**TS** *Three hundred years ago in London during the plague, the city was not a very sanitary place to live.* **PS** Londoners, both rich and poor, bathed infrequently. **PS** The city had no underground sewer system. **PS** Heaps of solid refuse sat around in the open.

**Secondary Support Sentences**                                                    **149**

Any sentence that further explains, argues, illustrates, or in any way elaborates upon or supports a primary support sentence is a **secondary support sentence**. Typically, these sentences provide the reader with detailed facts and specific examples that clarify the generalizations in the primary support sentences. The secondary support sentences also make the paragraphs more interesting.

*Examples*

## 1

**TS** *Marvel comics were most interesting and realistic because of the constant change they all exhibited.* **PS** For example, the character relationships were not static. **SS** New characters were added; old characters were dropped; bad guys became good guys, and good guys became bad guys. **SS** Marvel characters appeared in each others' books as much as they did in their own. **SS** In Marvel comics the characters matured and aged as time passed. **SS** Spiderman and the Human Torch both graduated from high school and attended college. **SS** (Robin, the Boy Wonder, has been an adolescent for decades.) **SS** Mr. Fantastic and the Invisible Girl were married and even had a baby. **SS** Superman has dated Lois Lane for fifty years. **SS** Death is not uncommon in Marvel comics, as the Human Torch's father died, and so did Sergeant Fury's girlfriend. **SS** The good guys were even prone to lose at times, as in the Hulk vs. The Thing battle.

## 2

**TS** *Debbie finds the men who frequent the school cafeteria boring because, to her, almost all of those men fit too easily into one of three stereotyped groups.* **PS** The Blacks sit together at a double row of tables by the front doors. **SS** Of all the groups, this group seems to have the best time, talking, laughing, and listening to jazz on transistorized radios. **SS** Many of these students belong to the Black Student Union, and they limit discussions to talk about club activities and which teachers don't like Blacks. **PS** A second group, the veterans, sit at a long row of tables near the cash registers. **SS** These men are mostly in their late twenties or early thirties. **SS** Some of them are Vietnam War veterans, and others are retired Air Force men. **SS** This group talks constantly about their GI benefits. **PS** A third group, the cowboys, all lean their chairs against the west wall. **SS** These men, most of them young, wear cowboy hats, Western shirts, Levis with rodeo buckles, and muddy, manured cowboy boots. **SS** The majority of these students live or work on ranches outside of the city, and they major in agriculture. **SS** Very opinionated, this group—in general—hates marijuana smokers (cowboys sniff snuff and drink beer), farmers, Volkswagens, and suburbia. **SS** The favorite topics of discussion in this area of the cafeteria are pickup trucks and guns.

## 3

**TS** *Three hundred years ago in London during the plague, the city was not a very sanitary place to live.* **PS** Londoners, both rich and poor, bathed infrequently. **SS** Most families bought a limited amount of water daily from waterbearers, and there were no private baths. **SS** Samuel Pepys wrote in his secret diary that his wife actually dared to wash herself all over at a public "hothouse" and that a few days later he bathed also, an unusual event. **PS** The city had no underground sewer system. **SS** Instead of sewers, kennels (open gutters) were used for waste liquids from chamber pots and wash-up water. **SS** The evil-smelling liquid trickled along until it reached the River Thames. **PS** Heaps of solid refuse sat around in the open. **SS** Solid human waste, garbage, and other refuse was heaped in the courtyard or dumped in the street to be carried away by the parish "raker." **SS** On irregular visits the raker collected the waste in his cart and took it to one of the laystalls (refuse dumps and dung heaps) at the outskirts of London near the river bank.

**150**

## Primary and Secondary Support Clusters

As you can readily observe in the example paragraphs above, primary and secondary support sentences work together in **clusters**. A cluster begins with a *primary support sentence* and continues with one or more *secondary support sentences.* Each cluster—two, three, or more sentences—helps the reader comprehend the topic sentence. The primary support sentence that introduces the cluster owes its allegiance to the topic sentence, but each secondary support sentence in the cluster owes its allegiance to its primary support sentence.

## EXERCISE 3

How many support clusters did the writers include in example paragraphs #2 and #3 on page 150? (Answers on page 165)

1. Example 2 has _____ clusters.
2. Example 3 has _____ clusters.

## EXERCISE 4

In the following paragraph, place **TS** in front of the *topic sentence*, **PS** in front of each *primary support sentence*, and **SS** in front of each *secondary support sentence.* (Answers on page 165)

_____ No matter where Americans go, they are confronted with drugs. _____ Drug companies across the country advertise their products in magazines, on television, and on billboards. _____ Anacin is the aspirin "more doctors recommend"; Contac releases "hundreds of tiny time capsules"; "Use Sominex when you have trouble going to sleep." _____ Moreover, local pharmacies and supermarkets, regularly visited by every member of the family, advertise drugs in sale ads and in store displays. _____ Signs in stores promise that Cope will help people get through a tension-filled day. _____ Other display signs insist that the host or hostess who serves Smirnoff vodka will become the happiest, most popular person on the block. _____ If, however, people escape being influenced by the advertisements, they will almost certainly not escape social pressure. _____ When surrounded by people who drink alcoholic beverages, smoke tobacco, and drink coffee and tea with enthusiasm, one finds it difficult not to go along with the crowd.

## What If You Have Difficulty Labeling Sentences?

What is important in developing body paragraphs is that you explain yourself thoroughly. Labeling the sentences, although useful, is of secondary importance. Sometimes you will find it difficult to label the sentences in one of your paragraphs as being either *primary* or *secondary.* This difficulty does not necessarily mean that the paragraph is poorly organized or inadequately developed. In the following paragraph, for instance, the primary and secondary support sentences are not distinct; yet the paragraph is effective.

*When plague came to a London house in 1665, it was sealed by the law.* A watchman guarded the house to see that no one escaped. Both the sick and the well of the household were forced to stay inside during the forty days of quarantine. For the duration of that period, food and other necessities were delivered. A red cross was painted on the door of the household with the plague. A sign saying "Lord have mercy on us" was painted or nailed on each door doomed with the malady. The quarantine was extended as members developed the disease. If no one else showed symptoms during the forty days, a white cross replaced the red one. The white cross remained for twenty days. Meanwhile, the home was thoroughly cleaned, filled with fumes of burning sulphur, and coated with lime before it was declared free of infection.

## Paragraph Length

How long should a body paragraph be? *Any body paragraph that does not contain at least* **five sentences** *should be filled out with more secondary support sentences or expanded by adding one or more support clusters.* One, two, three, and four-sentence paragraphs belong in newspapers and magazines, where the columns are narrow, *not* in academic compositions.

Occasionally in a *long* composition you can use a very short paragraph for *transitional* purposes when you are linking major sections within the body of the paper. But no need exists for short transitional paragraphs in the compositions you will write while completing this book.

In general, long paragraphs are better than short ones, but *paragraphs can be too long*. For example, a paragraph that runs two or three pages in a handwritten paper may be difficult to read, just as a paragraph more than a page long in a typed composition can be hard to follow. When body paragraphs are too long, readers lose their trains of thought—their minds wander, and their eyes crave the sight of an *indentation* marking a new paragraph, a place to pause and rest and, perhaps, to reflect upon what has been said. For most compositions, body paragraphs that contain **five to ten sentences** seem very readable.

### Example

Both opponents and proponents of the death penalty would like to see televised executions. Those opposed to the death penalty think that if supporters of capital punishment were allowed to see an execution, they would realize the inhumanity of the act. By seeing a person electrocuted, hanged, gassed, shot, or drugged to death, the advocates of the death penalty might be moved to think again about the morality of their position and move to have capital punishment abolished. Advocates of the death penalty, however, hope that a public execution every now and then would act as an added deterrent to crime, that is, boosting the fear of punishment for those prone to commit felonious acts such as murder, kidnapping, and hijacking. By showing executions live on television, the potential felon might experience a more realistic fear of the consequences.

(5 sentences)

The body paragraph that follows *lacks sufficient development.* Expand and fill out the paragraph by adding primary and secondary support sentences. The revised version should be between *five and ten sentences* long.

Inflation causes serious problems for the American family. Prices keep rising. The prices of new homes, for example, have risen sharply. Because dollars buy less, people are forced to spend more to maintain a status-quo standard of living instead of saving money for better things.

Have your paragraph checked.

This paragraph is *too long*. Edit it, selecting the sentences that you want to keep, so that it will be no longer than *ten sentences* but not shorter than *five sentences*. Remember that you will need both *primary support sentences* and *secondary support sentences*. Feel free to change the wording in any of the sentences.

There is an old saying that people are what they eat. If that is the case, the students who eat in Thompson Hall at this university are in bad shape. The cafeteria should be the cleanest place on campus because of its importance to the health of all the students who eat there, but instead, it seems to be the dirtiest place for a student to eat. The cafeteria, along with the roaches and bugs, has a foul odor that seems to linger in the air. The smell of the food and the garbage does not produce an appetizing atmosphere in which to dine. Most of the odor is created because the cafeteria's disposal system is not up to par. The workers are very slow at emptying the trays and plates. That is one of the reasons the cafeteria runs out of glasses and silverware during breakfast, lunch, and dinner. Most of the time the eating utensils are unclean, whether washed or not. Food is left on the trays and silverware after washing, and detergent is left inside the glasses. Sometimes the dishwasher is broken, and at other times there is no detergent. If there is anything worse than the dirty dishes, it has to be the food. The food in Thompson Hall is more than terrible: it is ridiculous! There is no telling what might be served, from spoiled food to insects. Most of the food is cold—the food that is supposed to be hot, that is. The food that is supposed to be cold is warm. The milk is sour, and the bread is stale. The food is not cooked properly; either it is overdone and hard, or it is undercooked and tough. The menu is never properly balanced; some days they serve too much starch and fat, and they never provide enough protein food. To pay $112.50 for a meal book each semester and not be able to get a good balanced meal is absurd. This problem needs to be investigated as soon as possible.

_____

_____

_____

_____

_____

_____

_____

_____

_____

_____

_____

Have your work checked.


## The Importance of Details

More than anything else, every body paragraph needs pertinent **details**. Your instructor expects detailed discussion, not a series of unsupported generalizations. You may know what you mean when you make a generalization, but you cannot be certain your reader will know what you are thinking, unless you explain your ideas thoroughly. Of course, easy-to-follow organization helps. Begin each body paragraph with a topic sentence, and support the topic sentence with a clearly organized pattern of primary and secondary support sentences (support clusters). But to write detailed paragraphs, you must make a special effort to include enough secondary support sentences. When you add _explanations, examples, quotations, statistics, anecdotes, and other kinds of specifics_, you increase the chances that your reader will understand—and believe—what you are trying to say.


## Support Your Generalizations with Specifics

In the following illustrations of _secondary support sentences_, the topic sentences and primary support sentences have been stripped away so you can more easily see how effective secondary support sentences are written. Notice that even though five different types of secondary support sentences are offered, they all have one thing in common: they give detailed, specific information about some topic.

1. Explain your ideas.

   Rising college costs are causing problems. This year a fresh group of parents and students must grapple with grim economic realities as admission notices arrive. Savings accounts are smaller, more inflation is almost certain, and competition for loans and scholarships is increasing.

2. Use examples.

> Johnson notes, for instance, that one of every three students filing for admission now asks for financial aid, compared with one of every four last year.

> For example, fewer students major in liberal arts programs to "learn how to work with people." But more students enroll in business and science programs.

3. Use facts and statistics.

> Both the University of California and the State University predict cost increases of at least twelve percent this coming academic year.

> At a public four-year campus, the report estimates tuition and fees will average $578, transportation $202, personal expenditures $454, room and board $1,272, and books and supplies $173.

> The sampling shows that fifty-five percent of the students eligible for graduation this June have completed Freshman Composition with a grade of C or better.

4. Use quotations.

> Warren stated, "A family must save almost two thousand dollars a year for nine years for each child planning to attend four years of college."

5. Use anecdotes (personal experiences).

> When I attended the University of Michigan, costs were much lower. Tuition, for example, was only $125 per semester.

> Yet we were always short of money and welcomed the summer vacations when we could replenish our depleted bank accounts.

**EXERCISE 7**

For each *generalization* that follows, add a *secondary support sentence* that contains the type of *specific details* requested. You may invent the fact, figures, quotations, and other kinds of details you are asked to use.

1. Many students attend school part time because they have jobs.

(Explanation) _____

_____

_____

_____

2. Fashions of dress are always changing for both men and women.

(Examples) _____

_____

_____

_____

3. Due to the high cost of new homes, the majority of newly married couples will soon live in apartments and other types of multiple housing units.

(Facts and statistics) _____

_____

_____

_____

4. A serious shortage of natural gas for industry and homes is imminent.

(Quotation) _____

_____

_____

_____

5. This school has changed.

(Anecdote—personal experience) _____

_____

_____

_____

_____

Have your sentences checked.

## EXERCISE 8

In the following paragraph, the secondary support sentences have been omitted. Complete *each cluster* by adding one or more *secondary support sentences*.

**TS** Jane decided to attend college for three very important reasons. **PS** She wanted to meet new and interesting young men. **SS** (one or more)

_____

_____

_____

_____

_____

**PS** She also knew that a college education would be required if she were to become a microbiologist. **SS** (one or more)

_____

_____

_____

_____

_____

**PS** Although all other reasons for going to college were important, the most important was that all her friends decided to attend college. **SS** (one or more)

_____

_____

_____

_____

_____

Have your sentences checked.


### Where To Find the Specifics You Need

Where do you find these specific details? You can find the information you need in books, magazines, pamphlets, lecture notes, on television, in movies, interviews, and discussions. However, the best source of supporting information is your own head. You know more than you might think you do. You have read; you have listened to others; you have lived and worked. Through all this experience you have been gathering ideas, opinions, and facts that you can use in your paragraphs. If you take the time to think, you can probably come up with most of the specifics you need to develop your ideas without consulting other sources.

### Be Reasonable, and Have Something To Say

Think through what you want to say in a sentence or cluster of sentences before you write it—or at least before you leave it. If your thinking is empty or muddled, so will be your writing. Try to be logical, and try not to overgeneralize. Do not tell the readers what they know already.

**158**

_Don't write—_
There are nothing but police dramas on television every day. (_overgeneralized_)

_Instead, write—_
Evening television is glutted with police dramas. (_more reasonable_)

_Don't write—_
Millions of Americans watch television. (_Your readers know this._)

*Write instead—*

A growing minority of Americans refuse to watch television except to see a few very special programs. (*Your readers might not know this.*)

or perhaps

I have not watched a single television program for three weeks. (*Your readers, both those who watch television regularly and those who do not, will be interested in this statement and read on to find out why.*)

Just sit and think a bit, or read a little; a visit to the library will produce ideas. With a small amount of effort—mostly thinking—you can utilize your knowledge of everyday experiences in such a way that the content of your paragraphs will become interesting and worthwhile for your readers.

**EXERCISE 9**

The statements below are *overgeneralized*, or they merely *say what everyone already knows.* Rewrite them so they will be more effective.

1. Welfare recipients are all a bunch of cheaters.

_____

_____

_____

_____

**159**

2. Television programs and movies are full of violence and sex.

_____

_____

_____

_____

3. Millions of Americans drive automobiles.

_____

_____

_____

_____

4. Everyone has the need to eat.

_____

_____

_____

_____

5. Almost every American woman hates being a housewife.

_____

_____

_____

_____

Have your work checked.

### Smoothly Connecting Sentences within the Paragraph

The sentences within a body paragraph should **connect smoothly** to one another. You can strengthen this coherence in a paragraph by using *transitional words and phrases*, repeated words, and other connectives and expressions that help your reader move from one idea to the next. You must also be careful to *arrange your sentences in order*; edit each body paragraph to remove irrelevant sentences and to move any sentences that seem to be in the wrong place. (Some specific organizational strategies you can use will be covered in the next unit.) Finally, a variety of sentence patterns should be used. The sentences should not all be simple or compound or complex. A combination of sentence patterns that will enhance the orderly progression of ideas should be built, either during the initial writing or as the result of revision. Study the paragraph below to see how the author has made the sentences flow together. Some of the words and phrases that contribute to this coherence are italicized.

160

*Example*

Sometimes the truth cannot be told. *In wartime, for example,* political and military leaders must often weigh one evil against another, *and* frequently the virtue of telling the truth *gives way to* the necessity of *some greater good. It is well known that* during World War II the city of Coventry in England was devastated by a German bombing raid. *What is not generally known is that* the British *high command* knew through cracking the Germans' communications code that this was going to happen. *If, however,* the British had mounted a defense of Coventry, the Germans would have realized that their code was broken, would have changed the code, *and, thus,* would have denied the Allies' intelligence vital to the success of the Normandy invasion, which was then on the drawing board. The *high command, therefore,* had to conceal what they knew and allow the tragedy of Coventry, for the *greater good* of preserving their plan to make an end to the war and the suffering of whole nations.

### Concluding Sentences

A body paragraph may need a **concluding sentence** that will bring the paragraph to a close. Not every paragraph needs one, but some seem to leave the reader ''hanging'' because the paragraph ends abruptly. A concluding sentence can state a conclusion, summarize what has been said, or point toward the next paragraph. Strictly speaking, this sentence is neither a primary support sentence nor a secondary support sentence because it is not a developmental or support sentence. The concluding sentence in the previous sample paragraph, for example, summarizes and states the author's conclusion.

The high command, therefore, had to conceal what they knew and allow the tragedy of Coventry, for the greater good of preserving their plan to make an end to the suffering of whole nations.

### EXERCISE 10

Rewrite the paragraph below so that the sentences will *connect more smoothly.* (Not more than ten sentences )

Scientific evidence is mounting. Too many Americans do not eat right. Today's diet apparently is the cause of numerous nutrition-related problems. Too many Americans eat too many calories. They do not expend enough energy. Most Americans become overweight. They eat too much animal protein, saturated fat, and cholesterol. Too many people develop heart disease. They also eat too much refined sugar and starch. They do not eat enough complex carbohydrates. Such as whole grain cereal and bread. And they develop metabolic disorders. Such as diabetes. They do not eat enough crude fiber either, such as vegetables, and they develop many diseases, such as diverticulosis and cancer of the colon. Americans must reconsider their eating habits.

_____

_____

_____

_____

_____

_____

_____

_____

_____

_____

_____

_____

_____

_____

**EXERCISE 11**

Write a *concluding sentence* for the paragraph that follows.

The fast-food business, which has become increasingly prevalent on Maui in recent years, seems to depend heavily on advertising gimmicks for its popularity. Each food chain tries to outdo the others in catchy phrases, appeals to the stomach and pocketbook, and promotional specials. MacDonald's, for instance, probably has the slickest television ads and always seems to be coming up with something new. Their "Good morning, America" ads for a fast, nutritious, economical breakfast have lately been replaced by a series about the "Big Mac Attack," in which the excellence of their Big Mac hamburger can even whet the appetite of an empty suit of armor. Another example is the familiar face of Colonel Sanders hawking his Kentucky Fried Chicken on the television networks. The gimmick here seems to be that the Colonel is the epitome of the gracious South, and, of course, everyone knows that Southern fried chicken is the best. Discount coupons appearing frequently in the newspapers make it even harder to resist the "Finger lickin good" chicken, crispy or regular.

**162**  Concluding sentence  _____

_____

_____

_____

Have your sentence checked.

# Unit Five Practice Test

**Part One**. Place **TS** in front of each *topic sentence*, **PS** in front of each *primary support sentence*, **SS** in front of each *secondary support sentence*, and **CS** in front of each *concluding sentence* (not every paragraph has one). Answers on page 165.

1. _____ The rock music of the lates sixties and the early seventies evolved from the blues. _____ Every musician who made it to the top of the rock scene during that era has said that somewhere along the line he listened to or played the blues. _____ Eric Clapton, Jimi Hendrix, Johnny Winter, Alvin Lee, Michael Bloomfield—the list of superstars goes on and on—all played the blues. _____ Jimi Hendrix, for example, started a band and played in the South, where he first played the blues when he was seventeen years old. _____ When he first started out, Eric Clapton often listened to Robert Johnson. _____ Others who influenced Eric Clapton were Tampa Red and Blind Willie McTell. _____ Bloomfield, Lee, and Winter were also very much "into" blues. _____ They, too, listened very closely to these old blues players, and the results are reflected in their songs. _____ The blues influence on these rock players has in turn been carried into the rock and jazz of the late seventies.

2. _____ Because of the complexity of the world overpopulation problem and the length of time it takes to affect fertility rates, the planning and initiation of international programs cannot wait until the population explosion becomes more acute. _____ According to John Strohm, "The runaway population has jumped from two to four billion people in just 45 years, a 'doubling' that used to take hundreds or even thousands of years." _____ Many think that some technological miracle will solve the population problem. _____ Technology may help solve the problem, but it is not a substitute for programs of population growth control that should be introduced now. _____ An increasing awareness of population trends and their implications is causing a growing number of nations to take action. _____ India, Pakistan, Egypt, Tunisia, Korea, and Japan have formulated population policies and are developing programs to make sure that the Malthusian checks to population—vice, misery, famine, and war—do not provide the solution to their growing hordes of people. _____ When any nation today looks carefully at its need for food, housing, schools, hospitals, and jobs over the next fifteen years, it cannot avoid seeing the crisis at hand.

**Part Two**. Write a *body paragraph* on any topic. (You may want to develop one of the topic sentences written for Exercise 12 in Lesson 6 of Unit Four on page 138.) Label the topic sentence **TS** , each primary support sentence **PS** , each secondary support sentence **SS** , and the concluding sentence **CS**. (Perfect the paragraph on notebook paper before copying it in your book.)

_____

_____

_____

_____

**164**

Have your work checked.

# Answers for Unit Five Exercises

**Exercise 1 (page 147)**

5

**Exercise 2(page 148)**

1 and 3

**Exercise 3 (page 151)**

1. 3
2. 3

**Exercise 4 (page 151)**

*TS* No matter where Americans go, they are confronted with drugs. *PS* Drug companies across the country advertise their products in magazines, on television, and on billboards. *SS* Anacin is the aspirin "more doctors recommend"; Contac releases "hundreds of tiny time capsules"; "Use Sominex when you have trouble going to sleep." *PS* Moreover, local pharmacies and supermarkets, regularly visited by every member of the family, advertise drugs in sale ads and in store displays. *SS* Signs in stores promise that Cope will help people get through a tension-filled day. *SS* Other display signs insist that the host or hostess who serves Smirnoff vodka will become the happiest, most popular person on the block. *PS* If, however, people escape being influenced by the advertisements, they will almost certainly not escape social pressure. *SS* When surrounded by people who drink alcoholic beverages, smoke tobacco, and drink coffee and tea with enthusiasm, one finds it difficult not to go along with the crowd.

**Unit Five Practice Test (page 163)**

1. *TS* The rock music of the late sixties and the early seventies evolved from the blues. *PS* Every musician who made it to the top of the rock scene during that era has said that somewhere along the line he listened to or played the blues. *SS* Eric Clapton, Jimi Hendrix, Johnny Winter, Alvin Lee, Michael Bloomfield—the list of superstars goes on and on—all played the blues. *SS* Jimi Hendrix, for example, started a band and played in the South, where he first played the blues when he was seventeen years old. *SS* When he first started out, Eric Clapton often listened to Robert Johnson. *SS* Others who influenced Eric Clapton were Tampa Red and Blind Willie McTell. *SS* Bloomfield, Lee, and Winter were also very much "into" blues. *SS* They, too, listened very closely to these old blues players, and the results are reflected in their songs. *CS* The blues influence on these rock players has in turn been carried into the rock and jazz of the late seventies.

2. TS Because of the complexity of the world overpopulation problem and the length of time it takes to affect fertility rates, the planning and initiation of international programs cannot wait until the population explosion becomes more acute. *PS* According to John Strohm, "The runaway population has jumped from two to four billion people in just 45 years, a 'doubling' that used to take hundreds or even thousands of years." *PS* Many think that some technological miracle will solve the population problem. *SS* Technology may help solve the problem, but is is not a substitute for programs of population growth control that should be introduced now. *PS* An increasing awareness of population trends and their implications is causing a growing number of nations to take action. *SS* India, Pakistan, Egypt, Tunisia, Korea, and Japan have formulated population policies and are developing programs to make sure that the Malthusian checks to population growth—vice, misery, famine, and war—do not provide the solution to their growing hordes of people. *CS* When any nation today looks carefully at its need for food, housing, schools, hospitals, and jobs over the next fifteen years, it cannot avoid seeing the crisis at hand.

# UNIT SIX
# *Paragraph Strategies*

## *Objectives*

After completing this unit, you will be able to

1. create *interesting illustrations* for paragraphs.
2. use *factual detail* for paragraph illustration.
3. employ *anecdotes* for paragraph illustration.
4. compose *extended-definition* paragraphs.
5. write *comparison* or *contrast* paragraphs.
6. compare through *analogy.*
7. organize *chronological, structural,* and *cause-and-effect paragraphs.*
8. revise and proofread paragraphs.

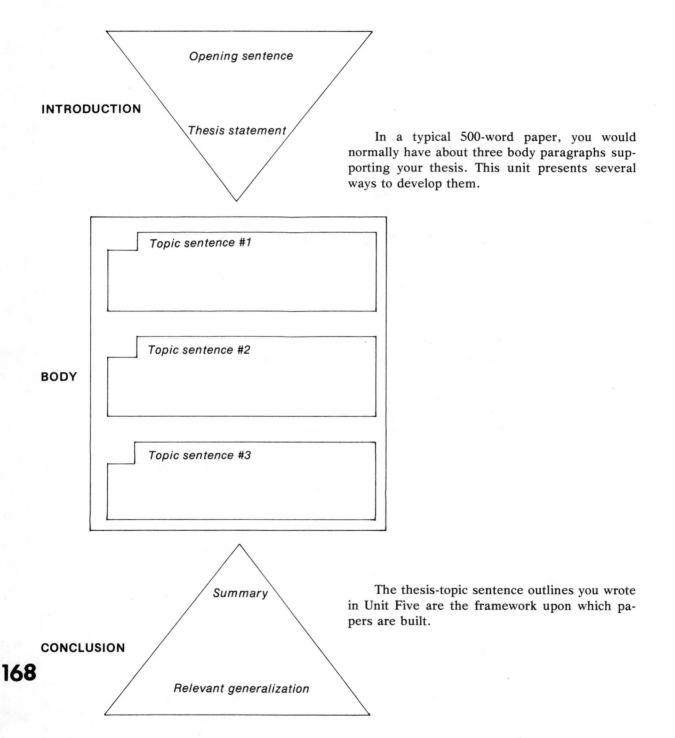

**INTRODUCTION**

*Opening sentence*

*Thesis statement*

In a typical 500-word paper, you would normally have about three body paragraphs supporting your thesis. This unit presents several ways to develop them.

**BODY**

*Topic sentence #1*

*Topic sentence #2*

*Topic sentence #3*

**CONCLUSION**

*Summary*

The thesis-topic sentence outlines you wrote in Unit Five are the framework upon which papers are built.

*Relevant generalization*

**168**

# 6

Having mastered topic, primary-support, and secondary-support concluding sentences, you are now ready to begin writing carefully structured body paragraphs that will communicate exactly what you wish to say. As you select topics about which to write, consider hobbies, work, and television. Provided you begin with a strong topic sentence, you can almost certainly develop a paragraph on any of these subjects.

After selecting a subject and writing a topic sentence, what then? Of course, you must write primary and secondary support sentences, but not yet. First, you must decide what you want to do with the subject. That is, do you wish to illustrate a point, compare, or contrast two objects or ideas, define a term or concept, examine something, or argue a position? The impact you wish to create will determine how you write the paragraph, and because this approach is carefully planned, it is called *planning your strategy*. This planning will result in paragraphs that succeed because they are deliberate. Probably as a result of the deliberateness, the various paragraph types are called **paragraph strategies.**

When you have decided upon the purpose and plan of your paragraph, it is time to begin writing. Many people find that sketching their ideas on a piece of notebook paper can help them begin. If you decide to do this, you only need to write your topic sentence at the top and the points you expect to cover in each primary support sentence below that. Then, keeping that rough sketch before you, write the paragraph rapidly on another piece of paper, not worrying about errors. With that first draft of your paragraph completed, you can then reread to be sure you have correctly spelled all words, correctly punctuated all sentences, and included enough secondary support to completely illustrate what you intended to say in the primary support sentences. After you have completed all this, copy your work into the appropriate space in the book.

169

## LESSON ONE—The Illustration Strategy

The **illustration** paragraph, one of the easiest to write, allows the writer to fully explain the ideas presented in the topic sentence by giving *examples*. If you wish to write a paragraph in which you convince your reader that the national 55 MPH speed limit is good, you could illustrate your point with many examples. For instance, you might use examples to point out that fuel is saved, nerves are more relaxed, and lives are spared. because the lower speed limit was implemented. You could, of course, just as easily support the opposing point of view by using examples.

Any illustration paragraph will achieve maximum effectiveness only if it includes enough effective examples. These may be actual occurrences, specific examples, or statistical details, depending on the particular subject about which you are writing. However, as you write, remember to give extensive secondary support for every primary support sentence. Generally, the more secondary support you give, the clearer your point. As with all paragraphs, you should have *at least* five sentences; however, illustration paragraphs will normally achieve more power if you extend them to eight or ten sentences.

The following examples are typical illustration paragraphs which proceed deliberately from clearly stated topic sentences. *Paragraph A* uses two **short examples** to illustrate the point that "Individuals frequently have attempted to prove their theories through fantastic feats of daring." The individuals listed—Thor Heyerdahl and Neil Armstrong— and their feats are given as examples. *Paragraph B* also illustrates by example; however, this type of development would be classified as **extended example.** When writing a paragraph of this type, you give long, extended descriptions of an incident, technique, or object. Consider the following examples.

### A. Illustration—short examples

Individuals frequently have attempted to prove their theories through fantastic feats of daring. Often these people have tested their capabilities for endurance against powerful odds. Thor Heyerdahl, for example, has twice challenged the sea, once on *Kon-Tiki* and once on *Ra*, to prove that primitive man could have migrated across the ocean. Taking personal risks that might cower lesser persons, these daredevils have inspired the admiration of the world. For instance, Neil Armstrong took the long journey to the moon. His feat, undertaken to prove several theories, involved considerable personal risk, but it has earned for him a lasting place in history.

### B. Illustration—extended examples

The desire for "sex appeal" is one of the most successful approaches used in television commercials today. Men and women alike have a natural desire for perfection, beauty, and the gifts of charm and charisma. Needing to feel admired, wanted, and loved by the opposite sex, they believe that certain physical traits and prerequisites are necessary to taste the joys and happiness of living. Companies selling products realize this, resulting in the exploitation of this knowledge for their own advantage. Consider, for example, the Old Spice commercial which epitomizes the masculine man in the ruggedly handsome sea captain, certainly the typical "dreamboat" of every woman's fantasies. The commercial shows a scrawny, studious young man looking on enviously as a glamorous woman rushes eagerly to "her" man disembarking from his ship. Of course, all ends happily when the sea captain casually tosses a bottle of Old Spice to the young man, leaving the viewers with the unspoken promise that this aftershave lotion will conjure instant vitality and excitement into the young man's life. Serta's Joey Heatherton is a more blatant illustration of employing the desire for sex appeal in advertisements. Joey's low, husky voice, clinging gown, and sensuous movements caress the senses and imagination, having a tremendous effect upon the audience. She invokes provocative visions of pleasure and befitting delights to be enjoyed on a Serta bed. People remember the "sex appeal" products; those lingering memories make the advertisements a success.

170

**EXERCISE 1**

Write one *illustration paragraph* that you make clear and interesting through the use of well-chosen examples. Label the topic sentence **TS**, the primary support sentences **PS**, and the secondary support sentences **SS**. (Do your work on notebook paper, and copy the final draft in this book.) As you search for a topic, consider using one of your topics from Units Four or Five; recycling ideas often saves time when you are writing paragraphs.

Have your paragraph checked.

## Factual Details and Anecdotes

Two less commonly encountered kinds of illustration paragraphs—the **factual detail** and the **anecdote**—are occasionally used in special circumstances. When you illustrate a point by using facts and figures for supporting evidence, you would normally describe the result as an illustration paragraph using factual detail.

*Illustration—factual detail*

Many educators are concerned about the fact that children in the ghetto schools often tend to lose ground in IQ. Only 21.8 percent of Central Harlem Junior High School students are in special progress classes. That figure is relatively high compared to 13.4 percent in New York's predominately white district. Also, the statistics are high for drop-outs in the lower economic districts. One may find these statistics quite shocking. Of the 1,276 students from four Harlem junior high schools in 1970-72, less than half were graduated in 1972. Records were located for 1,012; 117 others transferred to other schools. Of the 1,012, 44.6 percent were graduated. Thus, quite obviously, ghetto schools are not doing a good job of educating their students, certainly not equally as well as the suburban schools.

An *anecdote*, a short story (narrative) that is frequently biographical or personal in nature, may also be used to illustrate a point. To write an effective anecdotal paragraph, always start with a strong, pointed topic sentence; then with the second or third sentence, begin the anecdote or personal account as in the paragraphs below. (Be cautious that anecdotal paragraphs you write do not become so lengthy that your reader forgets the idea presented in the topic sentence.)

*Illustration—anecdote*

To fully enjoy life, people must be able to adapt to situations that turn out differently than they had expected. It is this adaptability that can turn almost all thwarted plans into memorable experiences, regardless of unexpected problems. Recently, for example, when my lady and I drove to the Pacific Ocean for the final dive of our SCUBA class, we had been looking forward to seeing some beautiful underwater sights and enjoying a day's diving. However, as we began to prepare our equipment a few feet from the water's edge, we became aware of immense, crashing waves. Although we attempted to ignore these waves, we eventually became intimidated as other students were driven back onto the beach, equipment disheveled or lost, terror in their eyes. When our turn came, we backed, with awkward movements, down the beach and into the surf. When the swirling water became knee deep, we whirled and dropped into the water, just as we had been instructed. As an awesome, ten-foot wave came crashing toward us, we submerged, and the wave passed harmlessly over us. Repeatedly employing this technique, we arrived at the dive raft in near record time, breathless but ready to enjoy the underwater sights. Unfortunately, the water's turbulence left visibility only eighteen inches so that we could see nothing worth mentioning. Although we were disappointed by the poor diving and were tempted to drive home depressed, we took advantage of the situation by driving south along the coast road to witness and photograph some of the most spectacularly huge waves either of us had ever seen. We arrived, approximately mid-afternoon, at an isolated beach where we watched sea otters play in the surf while we ate a fantastic picnic lunch. While some apprehension remains about swimming through the surf's ferocity, we will never forget the beauty of that afternoon because rather than driving home in disappointment, we adapted to the situation at the ocean as we found it, and an enlarged color photograph of a particularly impressive wave now hangs on the living room wall.

The first person (personal pronoun), words like *I, we, our* and *they* may be used whenever the example is a personal experience being reported to illustrate a particular point. *Its use is to be avoided in any other way in expository writing.* In other words, **do not use** *I think, in my opinion,* or the like. (Avoid the second person *you* if possible. Occasionally, as in example 1 above, second person works better than either first or third person. In such an instance you can use second person. However, use it rarely and *only* in anecdotal paragraphs.)

**EXERCISE 2**

Write one paragraph using either *factual detail* or *anecdote.*

**173**

Have your paragraph checked.

## LESSON TWO—The Definition Strategy

Whenever you write a **definition**, whether a sentence, or a paragraph, or a whole paper, you attempt to explain what something *is* or what something *is like*. Most writers who are defining use specific illustrations to achieve this end. And many writers contrast examples of what something is or is like with examples of what something is not or is not like. Other writers turn to analysis when they want to define. No single formula exists for you to follow when organizing a definition, especially when you are writing a whole paper of definition. What is important is that you recognize the need to define: the need to make clear to the reader just what something is, and, oftentimes, just what something is not.

The following example on "Progress" is a body paragraph taken from a composition in which the author found it necessary to spend a whole paragraph defining the term *progress.* After giving a general definition in the first sentence, the writer prepares the reader in the second sentence for examples of what progress is as opposed to what progress is not by stating, "However, there is often confusion about what is progress and what is not progress . . ." And after these examples the writer cites examples of accomplishments that are false progress. Such a discussion needs both the examples of what progress is and the examples of what progress is not.

**Extended definitions,** definitions that take a paragraph or more (or even a whole paper) to develop, usually begin with the minimum definition possible, then use illustration, historical examples, comparison, and the like for fuller clarification.

*Extended Definition*

1

Progress is a movement toward desirable goals, such as improvement in the total well-being of human society, involving discernible advances in the enlightenment, prosperity, happiness, and security of mankind. However, confusion about what is progress and what is not progress often abounds. For example, progress has been made in agriculture. Farmers have learned better techniques in farming, and advanced modern equipment has made it possible to cultivate more crops and do it easier and faster. Progress has also been made in medicine. Doctors can now transplant practically any organ in the human body—even the heart, the most vital organ in the body. People have also seen progress in working conditions. People now have higher wages and work fewer hours than they did twenty years ago. Scientists have progressed in their search of the moon. Many astronauts have explored the moon and have returned with valuable information. On the other hand, many changes which some people call progress are actually setbacks. Faster moving cars enable more people to speed to their deaths every year. The grand network of freeways and superhighways which stretches across America actually enables millions of cars to pollute the air with their exhaust fumes. The numerous mass-production industries are polluting the lakes, rivers, and streams, as well as the air. Many lakes and streams which used to be recreation areas now have "no swimming" signs. In addition, the sonic boom of lightning-speed jets is deafening people. Although these changes are advancements of modern society, they are not progress because of the bad side-effects that accompany these changes. Therefore, progress can be defined as advances toward desirable goals that can only be good for humankind.

2

Passive resistance can be defined as a method of expressing one's opposition to a law, an action, or an idea, without the use of physical violence or force. It is

174

not a new idea—examples of passive resistance can be found all through human history. Early Christians, confronted with pagan Roman law, permitted themselves to be fed to wild animals rather than renounce their religious beliefs. At no time, however, did they attempt to dissuade their torturers through the use of force. During the Nazi occupation of France in World War II, French workers used this method to disrupt German construction of military projects. They allowed themselves to be led to work sites, but on arrival they merely sat quietly and refused to go to work. Even the threats of firing squads and food restrictions could not persuade these people to participate in a task they felt was immoral. Perhaps the strongest examples of passive resistance can be found in America, where, incidentally, the method can be extremely effective. One can hardly forget the television coverage of students blocking military trains simply by placing their bodies across the tracks. Of course, someone came and moved them off the tracks, and the trains eventually arrived at their destinations, but the entire nation had seen this expression of opposition to war demonstrated by its youth.

It is easy to go astray in a paragraph of definition, so you must be wary of certain pitfalls. You must avoid *defining in a circle*, using words that are themselves being defined.

*Example*

**Weak**

*Freedom* is the concept of each individual being *free*.

**Weak**

*Democracy* is a term that may be applied to any country that follows the *democratic process*.

**Better**

*Patriotism* is the devotion of one's life, finances and well-being for his country.

One final pitfall to avoid when writing definitions is using emotionally loaded words. They do not make the definition much clearer because they reveal your bias through your emotional appeal. Since the writer's intent should be to define terms rationally (through reason) and persuade the reader through logic, a blatant emotional appeal weakens the whole composition.

*For example*

    The Supreme Court, a group of *reactionary, rich old men*, should be abolished.

    The Supreme Court, a group of *wise, patriotic, God-fearing men*, should be supported.

When writing *definition paragraphs*, be sure to start with a topic sentence which tells the reader exactly what the point will be. In the preceding paragraph on "passive resistance," the topic sentence informs the reader that it is ". . . a method of expressing one's opposition. . . ." This places the subject in a particular class of methods, a very limited class wherein one expresses opposition. Every definition paragraph you write must begin with such a limited device in the topic sentence.

## EXERCISE 3

Write an *extended definition* of *ONE* of the following terms. You may consult reference works, if you wish, but write the definition in your own words.

| | |
|---|---|
| pacifist | socialist |
| love | male chauvinist |
| stereotype | tornado |
| scapegoat | prejudice |
| patriot | individualized teaching |

_____

_____

_____

_____

_____

_____

_____

_____

Have your paragraph checked.

## LESSON THREE—The Comparison or Contrast Strategy

In writing **comparison or contrast** paragraphs, a writer stresses how two or more things *are alike* or *how they are different*. The effectiveness of this type of paragraph is dependent upon how well it is organized. You must be certain, for example, that the point of comparison or contrast is made rather early and then developed in such a way that your reader does not have to jump about from one subject to another in some shotgun effect, random order. This can be highly confusing. Well-organized comparison or contrast paragraphs are a most effective strategy for dealing with two items.

*For example*

**Comparison**

Although they do not look remotely alike, Olympic sailboats and soaring planes are very much alike in some ways. The first similarity one would notice is the lack of comfort in rough weather. Stuffed in a cockpit barely large enough for a small child, the pilot of a soaring plane bounces around the sky like a child on a pogo-stick when the winds are strong. The sailor on a small Olympic sailboard finds the cockpit to his boat slightly larger, but hardly more comfortable. When the winds increase, the boat literally bounces from one wave to the next, hesitating only long enough to throw a fresh bucketful of water on the shivering sailor. But an even more surprising similarity is the method of propulsion—suction—which allows both to move in their respective elements. The soaring plane's curved wing tops, not the flat wing bottoms, create a suction that holds the craft up in the sky. In the same manner, the sailboat is pulled through the water by suction created when the wind rushes by the curved sails. The airfoil created by the curved wing on one and the curved sails on the other makes soaring and sailing very much alike.

**Contrast**

Alexander Hamilton and Thomas Jefferson were two of the most influential figures in the formation of the government of the United States under its new Constitution. Though they both advocated a brand new type of democratic government, they had different ideas. Hamilton, born the illegitimate son of a

West Indian merchant, became the leader of the Federalists. He argued for a strong national government, loose interpretation of the Constitution, protective tariffs, excise taxes, and a U.S. Bank; he favored England in foreign affairs and industry at home. Jefferson, on the other hand, was born into the Virginia planting aristocracy. He was an agrarian and became the leader of the Democratic-Republicans. He was for state's rights, strict interpretation of the Constitution, France in foreign affairs, agriculture in domestic affairs, and he opposed the Federalist ideas of taxation and banking. Due to the opposite views of Hamilton and Jefferson, the political party system in America was born.

You will be frequently asked to compare or contrast political figures, characters in novels, philosophical points or social ideas. The supporting evidence for these comparison or contrast paragraphs is usually developed through *illustrations* by using specific details, examples, or anecdotes.

The evidence for support in comparison or contrast paragraphs may be arranged in several ways. You may deal with two ideas, for instance, *by devoting the first four or five sentences to one idea and then the rest of the sentences to the next idea.* With this method you deal with each idea in a *block of sentences.*

*For example*

**Sentence Blocks**

Another disadvantage for American teenagers is the matter of the cost to learn a trade. They have to attend a two-year college or a trade school. Either way, they have to spend a considerable amount of money and valuable time to attend school to obtain the necessary knowledge and skill. It takes money to maintain a vehicle for transportation, money for gas, repairs, and car insurance. Also, their training cannot compete with on-the-job training. They will still lack the necessary experience that would guarantee them jobs. Most employers in the United States want experienced workers, even if they have to go as far as importing the necessary trained personnel from other countries. The German youths, on the other hand, start their apprenticeships with a small salary, which increases from year to year. This raise is usually sufficient to cover all expenses, provided they live thriftily. By the time they become seventeen and have passed their *Meisterprufung,* they are experts in their trades. They have no problems whatsoever in finding jobs. Usually they continue to work for their employers for considerably higher salaries.

Another method is to *alternate points of comparison or contrast several times in the paragraph.*

**Sentence-to-Sentence Alternating**

Although one could point out many similarities in the two systems, the educational differences were the most apparent. The school in the country had approximately seventy-five first-through-eighth-grade students. All eight grades were taught by the same teacher in one big room. Approximately five hundred students attended the city school. Each grade was taught by its own teacher in a separate room. In the country school the members of one class at a time would go to the front of the room to demonstrate their knowledge by individually reciting or writing their lessons on the blackboard. The other classes would be quietly doing their assignments at their desks. The teacher spent about twenty minutes with each grade, once in the morning and once in the afternoon. In the city school the teacher would do most of the demonstrations on the board, and the students, in general, were quite noisy unless they were singled out by questions from the teacher. Very few actual work assignments were done in the school. All assignments were done at home. The class would spend forty-five minutes on each subject, covering five subjects a day.

Another method is to *deal with the points of comparison or contrast in the same sentence.*

### Single Sentence

The difference between Democrats and Republicans is the conflict of liberalism and conservatism. Democrats are, in a word, freer with public funds; Republicans are, in another word, tighter. Conversely, Republicans are more alarmed at the prospect of inflation; Democrats care about it, too, but not all that much. They have more loyal supporters than do the Republicans among those classes in society that need a break in the form of unemployment checks, maternity benefits, and low-rent housing. They can, therefore, be expected to appropriate funds with less concern about where the money is to be found or what its distribution will do to the level of prices.

You have the same choice, or combination of choices, *with the complete composition* as you have within each separate comparison or contrast paragraph. You may deal with the two ideas in blocks of paragraphs; you may alternate the ideas from paragraph to paragraph; or you may deal with the ideas within the same paragraph.

### Analogy

A useful and unique type of comparison is the **analogy**. This type is especially helpful when you wish to deal with an idea that is unfamiliar to most of your readers but want to make the idea understandable to everyone. To do this, you must compare the difficult idea to a more familiar and understandable idea that has similar characteristics. In *Hamlet*, for example, death is compared to sleep. While death and sleep are obviously different, some of their characteristics are similar and helpful in understanding the more difficult concept. Consider the following analogies:

1

When in the process of becoming airborne, gooney birds are like bulls in a bullfighting arena. Both blindly crash into anything and everything that happens to be in the path of their charge. The bird's attempt to get airborne is not at all unlike the bull's attempt to get up sufficient momentum to destroy his adversary. Like the bull that requires a considerable distance to achieve his speed, the bird must have an incredible amount of room to get up airspeed. Further like the bull, the bird refuses to stop or alter course once the charge has begun. Granted, the gooney does not deliberately attempt to kill any human being in his path, but this is of little comfort to the person who is struck by five pounds of flying gooney. Moreover, like charging bulls, these beautiful birds have been known to crash into cars and trucks. Drivers have occasionally found it necessary to drive off the road to avoid a collision with a gooney that is attempting to lift off the ground. Such a comparison between goonies and bulls not only suggests similarities in action; it also suggests parallels in intelligence.

2

Drinking, a social game, is played by society. In this game all players must follow rules of conduct. Every time a player breaks these rules he receives an immaturity card. When a player acquires three immaturity cards, he is considered a social drinker, and at four, a frequent drinker. After five have been collected, he is considered a drunk and kicked out of the game. The winner is the one who receives the least number of immaturity cards without becoming a drunk.

**EXERCISE 4**

Write a paragraph of 100 to 150 words in which you develop by *comparison or contrast* one of the topics listed below.

1. Compare or contrast two political presidential candidates.
2. Contrast two instructors.
3. Compare or contrast the sexual, racial, foreign policy, or fashion attitudes of the present generation of young people with their parents' generation.
4. Develop an analogy (e.g., between college and business, war and Congress).
5. Contrast two viewpoints (e.g., on war, capital punishment, the draft, abortion).
6. Compare or contrast two kinds of automobiles.
7. Compare or contrast two ways to quit smoking.
8. Compare or contrast two modes of travel.
9. Compare or contrast two acquaintances.

**180**

Have your work checked.

# LESSON FOUR—The Analysis Strategy

When you wish to deal with a subject that is somewhat complex, you may choose to *divide it into various parts or classifications*. (Some instructors and texts will refer to this as paragraph development by *division* or paragraph development by *classification*.) **Analysis** divides the subject in some logical way, usually *chronological order* or *structural components*. As in the case of comparison and contrast, an analysis can consist of a single paragraph or a full-length composition.

## Chronological (Time Order) Analysis

When dealing with a process, *how* to make or *how* to do something, *time order* is important. Every effective analysis paragraph of this type must explain step-by-step how the procedure is accomplished beginning with the first step and ending with the last.

> Checking a crankshaft for cracks by the wet magnaflux method is a simple procedure. The first thing that must be done is to thoroughly clean and dry the crankshaft. This must be done because grease, dirt, oil, or water on the crankshaft will cause the magnaflux fluid to run off without indicating a crack, or it can cause a false crack indication. When it is clean and dry, the crankshaft can be loaded into the magnaflux machine where it is supported by rollers at each end with one end against a copper plate and an air cylinder at the other end. A large coil is then moved out from one support and moved along the length of the crank-shaft, stopping every two or three inches to energize the coil with an electric current. Simultaneously, magnaflux fluid is run over the shaft at the coil location. This fluid is a light oil with a magnetic fluorescent powder suspended in it. After the entire shaft has been covered, the coil is returned to the end and a large hood is lowered over the machine to darken the area. A black lamp is now used to inspect the crankshaft from one end to the other; at the same time the shaft is rotated to allow inspection of all sides, especially the fillet areas of the journals and the oil holes. This procedure will show up any cracks running around the crankshaft. These cracks will appear as white lines, varying from faint to bold depending on the depth of the crack. To check the crankshaft for longitudinal cracks, the air cylinder is activated, forcing a copper bar against the end of the crankshaft. Magnaflux fluid is then run over the crankshaft again, starting at one end and going to the other while simultaneously shooting a 2200 amp electric current through the crankshaft. The air cylinder is then released and the black-lamp is used to inspect for cracks running in a longitudinal direction on the journals and on the areas between the journals. Once the crankshaft has been inspected, direct contact is again made with the air cylinder and copper bar so that a decreasing current can be run through the crankshaft to remove any residual magnetism. The air cylinder is now released, the hood is raised, the shaft is removed from the machine, and the job is complete.

This strategy, *chronological order*, is useful, also, in writing about history.

## Structural Analysis

When you wish to divide a subject into parts, types, subtopics or elements to show the relationships between the parts, you must construct an *analysis of the structure* of the subject, thus *structural analysis*. This development could be used to analyze an atom, a paragraph, an automobile, a body, or for that matter, anything that has structure or parts.

Four types of American tourists are very conspicuous in Europe in the summer. One kind is the "See America First Tourist." Only rarely does this tourist venture outside of America, and when he does, he is always disappointed. He complains constantly that European scenery, historical sights, food, accommodations, and consumer products do not compare with those in America. He always wishes he could "find a good hamburger." Then there is the tourist who tries to be exactly like the natives. This traveler will go to almost any length to simulate the natives. He dons the same type of clothing the natives wear, eats the same kind of food, and if he survives long enough, he even tries to adopt the customs of the country being visited. This traveler is snobby about anything not absolutely "authentic." The third kind of tourist never goes anywhere without taking his camera equipment along. He is never seen without at least two cameras—one for still photos and the other for moving pictures—and many other photographic gadgets. He spends most of his time snapping away at famous landmarks and always includes his wife in each picture. The fourth type of tourist is the college-aged student. He hitchhikes or bicycles his way across Europe. He is characterized by an unkempt "hippie" appearance, knapsack, and Daddy's American Express credit card.

## EXERCISE 5

Develop one of the following subjects by *analysis* in a paragraph of 100 to 150 words. (You may need to do some research for the most effective development.)

1. Attitudes toward drugs, sex, or the military
2. Water pollutants
3. How to make something
4. Types of students who frequent the student center
5. Types of instructors
6. An historical event
7. Types of gasolines, oils
8. How to do something
9. Choose your own topic for analysis.

Have your work checked.

## LESSON FIVE—The Cause-and-Effect Analysis Strategy

When you want to deal with that information that connects two events, you will develop your paragraphs by **cause-and-effect analysis**. Essentially, it is the connection between the cause and its effect that will be the subject of your writing. For example, you might wish to explain in what way the causes of World War II are connected to the effects of that war. Or you might want to answer the questions, what are the causes of poverty, and how do its effects lead back to its causes?

Frequently, cause-and-effect paragraphs are the basis for a *whole composition* in which you attempt to persuade the reader of the wisdom or truth of your conclusions. At other times cause-and-effect compositions may be used simply to inform the reader of the connections.

Remember, causes and effects are linked, and it is that linking that is the primary subject in this type of development. Some kinds of development imply chronology or situation. Cause-and-effect development uses chronology or situation to get at the questions *what happened*, or *what happens*, or *what will happen*? Whenever you deal with any of these questions, you are dealing with *effects*. And whenever you explain *why*, you are dealing with causes. Absolute separation of causes and effects is not necessary. If you become unsure about what you are writing, just ask yourself, "Am I explaining *what happens* or *why*?" (or *why something happens*). If you are, your composition is developing according to plan—even though you cannot clearly separate all of the sentences that explain causes from those that explain effects.

*Cause-and-Effect Analysis*

1

When the *Argo Merchant* blindly ran aground on Nantucket Shoals in December, 1976, a series of traumatic events were initiated. The more serious effect from the standpoint of the sea creatures was the 6.3 million gallons of oil which spewed into the sea. Needless to say, this caused the death of an untold number of these creatures. Unfortunately, the oil which gushed from the broken hull of the ship also destroyed the eggs of future generations of sea life. From the view of many resort owners along the nearby coastline, the grounding began weeks of constant worry of economic disaster. Had the oil washed ashore, every beach, boat, and dock would have been rendered useless by the thick oil. But the most noteworthy and potentially best effect of the incident was the awakening of the public and the maritime authorities to the danger presented by these poorly constructed and haphazardly operated giant tankers. Provided that sufficient public pressure is applied in the future to continue research on better ways to control the merchant fleet, it is possible that fewer tanker disasters will occur.

183

Benzedrine, Dexedrine, and other "upper" drugs when used continually produce psychological and physical addiction. The habitual user must carry pills with him at all times to keep "wired up," or he may experience severe mental and physical letdown. Five milligrams of Dexedrine, for example, wear off in four to six hours, and if the user is caught away from home without his pills, he may suddenly feel weak, slightly nauseated, irritable, light-headed, head-achey, and insecure. If he tries to go a whole day or more without his pills, he may have headaches as the blood vessels in his brain dilate, fly off the handle at the slightest provocation, become extremely depressed and withdrawn, feel tired and lethargic, and imagine that people do not like him, or that they are plotting against him, or not treating him fairly. If he tries to go a week or so without his pills, he may experience an emotional breakdown and think he has the flu. When Johnny Cash and Roger Miller were addicted to Dexedrine, they were afraid to go anywhere unless they had dozens of pills with them. Roger Miller said that he had to take at least fifteen milligrams of Dexedrine to have the courage and strength to make it to the corner supermarket.

3

Ingesting refined sugar and caffeine adversely affects blood sugar levels. When too much refined sugar is consumed, the blood-sugar level sky-rockets temporarily. But after an hour or so the blood-sugar level drops to a level far lower than before the sugar was eaten. This condition is caused by the over-secretion of insulin by the pancreas. Caffeine also can cause low blood sugar; thus, anyone who just has a strong cup of coffee with a heaping teaspoon of sugar in it for breakfast may feel hungry and fatigued an hour or two after he drinks it. This rapid and continued fluctuating of blood pressure is not good for a person's organs.

**EXERCISE 6**

Develop one of the following topics into one or more paragraphs of 100 to 150 words using *cause-and-effect* development.

1. Auto safety
2. Teen-age marriages
3. College majors
4. Essay tests
5. World War I
6. Oil slicks
7. Welfare
8. Education
9. Your choice

_____
_____
_____
_____
_____
_____
_____
_____
_____
_____
_____
_____
_____
_____

Have your work checked.

## LESSON SIX—Revision

To be a good writer, you must be creative, imaginative, and thoughtful. You must also have self-discipline, pushing aside personal desires of the moment, and sit with pen in hand or before a typewriter and translate your innermost thoughts into sentences and paragraphs that will be meaningful to others. It is hard work, a tough occupation, a demanding avocation. But most of your time is not spent in this endeavor of creativity. The tedium comes in the next step in the process—**revising**. Your job, in reality, is thus: write, revise, rewrite, revise, rewrite, revise—and on and on until finally you feel you have done your best—and then *revise it one more time.*

The most common complaint college instructors have about student papers is that they lack development. This means they lack the rich detail that not only makes the work interesting to read but "proves" the writer's ideas. Lack of development is the failure to include appropriate *secondary support* for illustration.

As a writer, you should also cultivate the habit **now** of rechecking your written work for poorly written sentences. *Will the reader understand what you mean?* Reread your work. Read it aloud to someone. Make certain that it contains no *vague generalizations*

*You must . . . examine your writing.*

(broad, unclear statements). If it does, underline them for identification and revision. And make certain it contains no *awkwardly constructed sentences, no agreement problems, no sentence fragments, and no run-ons or comma splices.* And lastly, make certain all *spelling, punctuation, and capitalization* errors are corrected.

Revision is tedious, but without the revision most good writers would not have been successful. As a writer you must separate the creative process from the process of perfecting the work into final form. This allows you to linger over the revision without the threat of losing any ideas that could be forgotten if creation and revision were carried on simultaneously. You must develop an ability to examine your writing objectively, seeing it as a reader would. Look for ways to improve everything you write. Almost everything ever written could have been improved; your writing will be no exception. The secret of a successful writer is being able to identify and revise weaknesses in what has just been written. The following paragraph is an original, weak paragraph.

**Weak**

With the increase of all categories of crime, law enforcement has had to adjust to the needs of today. They have had to increase the size of their departments and initiate special training programs in an effort to check the spiraling growth of crime. All officers are not honest, of course, but most are. They have instituted intensified training programs in such fields as special weapons and tactics, narcotics, juvenile crime, and management of detention facilities. The specialized police departments have caused marked increases in arrest and detention of criminals. And more work. With these arrests came an increase in clerical work load arrest reports, booking reports, trial dates, and release reports all require processing. Also control and management of prisoners in the detention facilities become increasingly difficult due to the size of prison population. The ultimate goal of improved staff and facility being the rehabilitation of the majority of the prison population. Federal, state, and local governments have increased the size and staffs of their detention facilities to accommodate the increase in prison populations.

186

While this paragraph may appear "good enough" at first glance, a close examination reveals many faults that make it unacceptable. All who write, even professional writers, find errors such as these in whatever they write; no one consistently writes perfect paragraphs the first time. The mark of an accomplished writer, then, is not being able to write beautiful paragraphs the first time but being able to convert imperfect ones into acceptable ones that communicate clearly. The message should be obvious: you must develop an ability to see the weaknesses in what you write and a willingness to revise your writing until those weaknesses are eliminated.

**EXERCISE 7**

*Revise the weak paragraph above*, making sure you remove all fragments, run-ons, comma splices, sentence errors, and misspelled words. Then go back through the paragraph again looking for areas which are weak because of missing secondary support. When you have strengthened any weak areas, go through the paragraph again to look for sentences which are out of order, sentences which should be placed elsewhere in the paragraph or completely omitted.

_____

_____

_____

_____

_____

When you have finished, check your work against the revised paragraphs that follow. Your paragraph *will differ* from the suggested revision, but your revised paragraph should be similar. If your work differs markedly, discuss the differences with your instructor.

### Revision

With the increase of all categories of crime, law enforcement agencies have had to adjust to the needs of today. They have had to increase the size of their departments and initiate special training programs in an effort to check the spiraling growth of crime. The majority of these agencies, whether federal, state, or local, have had an annual personnel increase of between ten and fifteen percent. They have instituted intensified training programs in such fields as special weapons and tactics, narcotics, juvenile crime, and management of detention facilities. The specialized departments and training have resulted in marked increases in criminal arrest and detention. With these increased arrests came an increase in the clerical work load; arrest reports, booking reports, and release reports all require time to process. Also, control and management of the prisoners in the detention facilities become increasingly difficult due to the size of prison population. Federal, state, and local governments have increased the size and staffs of their detention facilities to accommodate this increase. The ultimate goal of these improvements is the prevention of crime and rehabilitation of criminals.

## EXERCISE 8

*Revise* the following paragraph. Read through to identify any fragments, run-ons, comma splices, sentence errors, and misspelled words. On the second reading, look for areas which are weak because of inadequate supporting evidence; add words or sentences wherever more secondary support is needed. Finally, read the paragraph one more time to be sure all secondary sentences are in the proper order so they support the correct primary sentence.

### Paragraph for Revision

The problem in Northern Ireland between Catholics and Protestants are not what the American public is told. In spite of what the press suggests, the Catholics are not denied the right to vote. In addition, Northern Ireland Catholics are not the majority of the population, denied the right to rule their country by a powerful minority. Such as that in South Africa. And the British soldiers did not come to the rescue of the Protestants as the press would have the public believe. In fact, the soldiers came to Northern Ireland to protect the Catholics and were welcomed as nights in shining armore when they first arrived only after they had been in that country for a few weeks were they called names by the Catholic

**188**

minority, indeed, the press would apparently like the American public to believe that the trouble in Northern Ireland developed simply because the Catholic people refused to give up their religion.

_____

_____

_____

_____

_____

_____

_____

_____

_____

_____

_____

_____

_____

_____

_____

_____

_____

_____

_____

_____

_____

_____

Have your revision checked.

# UNIT SEVEN
## The Introductory and Concluding Paragraphs

### Objectives

After completing this unit, you will be able to

1. write interesting opening sentences that lead to thesis sentences.
2. compose effective transition sentences that lead smoothly into thesis sentences.
3. identify several styles of introductory paragraphs.
4. revise ineffective introductions.
5. define and demonstrate an anecdote.
6. demonstrate sentence variety and the effective use of transitions.
7. create efficient concluding paragraphs.
8. compose relevant generalizations for ending concluding paragraphs.

# 7

So far you have learned to choose and narrow subjects, write thesis and topic sentences, and write several different kinds of body paragraphs. You now know how to construct all of the inner parts of a composition. You have learned, for example, that good body paragraphs develop from good thesis sentences and that topic sentences develop from some part of the thesis sentence. Moreover, you have learned that body paragraphs, in addition to having topic sentences, include primary and secondary support sentences. Each fully developed paragraph should include pertinent support and illustrative examples that indicate to the reader just what your point is. It is through a well-planned, effective structure that your compositions will best communicate your ideas. Now, in Unit Seven, the time has come to learn how to create the final portions of your compositions: the *introductory* and the *concluding paragraphs*.

Your introduction and conclusion are important parts of the complete composition. Like other sections, each of these has its own set of structural characteristics that, with some variety, should be followed for the best results. Your **introduction**, for example, is the *most critical part of the composition*. It contains "the hook," the **opening sentence,**

especially constructed *to lure your reader's interest*, beyond which he might not read unless it is well written and provocative. Also, the introduction contains, at its end, the **thesis**: *the single most important sentence in the paper.*

Finally, your conclusion wraps up all your ideas into one final summation. A counterpart to the introduction, the concluding paragraph is your last chance to review and reaffirm the main ideas covered in the paper. In this way the reader is left with a good overall impression of the composition. Since people remember best what they read last, the significance of an effective concluding paragraph must not be underestimated.

The introduction and the conclusion suggest both the direction and the scope of the body of your paper and hold it tightly to its subject. While a strong introduction and conclusion probably will not do much to aid a weak body, an otherwise effective composition can be seriously marred by a weak introduction and conclusion. Consequently, you should master their construction well, for you will need to demonstrate how to put the whole composition together in Unit Eight. Even more important, you will be expected to effectively introduce and conclude all of your compositions in the future.

## LESSON ONE—How to Start It All

Most successful writers begin compositions by constructing the thesis statement, as you did in Unit Four. Some then proceed to write the body of the paper next. Only after completing the body do these writers compose a conclusion and finally an introduction to precede the thesis sentence. However, more typically perhaps, other writers, after completing the thesis statement, proceed directly to the development of the remainder of the introductory paragraph. Their thinking is that writing the portion of the introduction that precedes the thesis requires them to selectively narrow their focus of the subject to the point where they are ready to begin the body of the paper immediately; furthermore, this process helps prevent their ideas from wandering off the subject. If you follow the practice of these successful writers, you will probably be ready to begin writing the introductory paragraph as soon as you have developed your thesis statement.

The successful introduction, in addition to attracting your reader's attention and narrowing the focus of your paper, must establish the background for the ideas that follow. In brief form, the introduction outlines the content to be covered in the body of the paper. The initial statement starts in this direction by beginning with an interesting, yet broad **opening sentence.**

*Example*

Play is the work of children.

After arousing the reader's curiosity to read further, the introductory paragraph then progressively narrows the scope of the opening sentence's idea until it culminates with the last sentence in the paragraph: **the thesis statement.** This narrowing of a general subject establishes the direction the subject is to take in the rest of the paper. For example, the writer of the following paragraph has something very particular in mind, and each succeeding sentence comes closer to the specific point she is developing.

Play is the work of children. It is the method by which they order their experiences and so give meaning to events in their lives. Toys are the tools which facilitate learning. Most parents buy toys they hope will help their children

194

to grow emotionally and intellectually. But American toy manufacturers have warped this natural selection process by manipulating children's tastes and intimidating parents' judgments through persuasive television advertising. Millions of dollars have been spent to promote toys that are actually harmful to the developing values of children. The fashion dolls epitomize this corporate "rip-off" of American values. *Barbie and Dawn are two plastic young ladies who convey to children that superficial sexiness, consumer faddism, and female competitiveness are positive values.*

In the paragraph above, the thesis sentence informs the reader that the composition will maintain that Barbie and Dawn, two plastic dolls, are teaching children poor values. By contrast, the opening sentence begins with the very general comment that "Play is the work of children." The second sentence narrows the discussion of children and playing by observing that children learn by playing. From that sentence on, the paragraph limits the concept of learning through playing until the thesis specifies the poor values taught by Barbie and Dawn.

By allowing the first sentence to be general and then making the next three or four sentences lead to your thesis statement, the reader will see that your thesis is a logical outgrowth of your ideas.

*Review*

1. Opening sentence should attract reader interest
2. Middle sentences should lead reader toward thesis
3. Thesis should be logical outgrowth of preceding sentences.

A variation of this basic introductory form may be used when you want to give your readers some necessary background information before they read the body of your paper. This type of development may be used whenever your subject is likely to be unfamiliar to your readers. For example, you would probably not need background material if you were planning to discuss air pollution in Los Angeles: almost every knowledgeable reader knows something about the subject. However, for a subject that is not generally known, background information is desirable. For instance, since few readers know about the struggle between the United States Navy and the gooney birds on Midway Island, the writer of the following paragraph needs to give readers some background at the outset of the paper.

Two hundred and fifty thousand gooney birds have defeated the United States Navy for the past thirty years. The conflict began when the Navy decided the birds were endangering airplanes landing and taking-off from the airstrip on Midway Island. The birds have lived on the island for centuries and are unable to understand why they should no longer fly in the vicinity of the airfield; consequently, numerous mid-air collisions between gooneys and airplanes occur. To date there have been no airplane crashes as a result of these collisions, but the possibility of a tragic accident is ever present. Logically, the United States Navy decided to force the beautiful but clumsy birds to move to another island. Unfortunately for the Navy, the birds absolutely refuse to cooperate, and although the Navy has tried many frightening techniques, the birds still soar above the island. The continuing conflict between the United States Navy and the gooney birds of Midway Island illustrates the strength of the bird's determination to remain on the island of their birth.

195

In this paragraph the reader is told before he gets to the thesis why the Navy would want to rid the island of the birds and why the birds are reluctant to leave.

> Note: Introductory paragraphs, like the others in a composition, should have at least **five** sentences.

## EXERCISE 1

Write an *introductory paragraph* for a 500 to 1,000 word composition. After you have chosen a subject from the list of possibilities, narrow it down to a thesis statement. When you are satisfied with the thesis, write your paragraph on scratch paper and revise it until you have done your very best. Then copy your paragraph on the following page and submit it for evaluation. (Do not write the whole composition—just the introductory paragraph.)

Suggested General Subjects

1. Marriage
2. Television advertising
3. Solar energy
4. Smoking
5. Sports

General Subject Chosen:

_____

Possible Topics:

1. _____

2. _____

3. _____

Limited Topic: _____

_____

_____

Thesis Statement: _____

_____

_____

_____

_____

_____

Introductory Paragraph: _____

_____

_____

_____

_____

_____

_____

_____

_____

_____

_____

_____

_____

_____

_____

_____

_____

_____

_____

_____

_____

_____

**197**

_____

_____

Have your work checked.

# LESSON TWO—Other Ways to Start

While in Lesson One, you practiced writing one kind of introduction; you should also be familiar with other ways to write a composition's first paragraph. Some instructors might list a dozen or more ways to begin, but mastering a few introductory variations should be sufficient for most situations. Remember, a good beginning is critically important in attracting your reader's attention as well as in laying the foundation for your paper.

## Introductory Techniques

### 1. *An Anecdote*

An *anecdote*, a short narrative telling an interesting or amusing incident, is a favorite way to gain audience attention in speech openings and may be equally effective for the writer. Anecdotes are usually told to make or support a point. The following example, while it tells a story and is immediately interesting, suggests the writer's general area of concern. The thesis statement then indicates the relevance of the anecdote and the main idea of the paper to follow.

When the nude model was late for her session with the advanced art class, the instructor was irritated with the interruption to his instruction. After arriving a half hour late, she readily agreed to pose for the next class also rather than lose any wages. The next class, however, was beginning art, and the students had painted only vases and bowls of fruit. Without warning to the beginning class, the model stood on the platform in the middle of the circled double art tables and shed her robe. Although the class members who were on time were surprised, the real shock could be viewed on the faces of the late arrivals. Each young woman who came through the door during the next ten minutes caught her breath, blushed, and walked briskly to an art table with another woman (quite unlike normal behavior). Each young man did a "double-take" quickly checked the room number to assure no mistake had been made, cast eyes to the floor, and did not again look up until art paper was in place and brush was in hand, all done with a pseudo air of sophistication. Although the sexual revolution has been widely touted by the press and television, this incident illustrates that the average young person remains at heart quite conventional in attitudes toward love, marriage, and sex.

Remember, however, that the anecdote and the thesis must be closely related.

### 2. *A Statement of Fact*

A *statement of fact*, such as in the gooney bird paragraph in Lesson One may be used to inform the reader as well as interest him. This statement is especially effective if the facts are striking or dramatic.

Nearly all major research into learning theory indicates that positive reinforcement is far more effective than punishment. Experimentation with both animal and human subjects reveals that punishment is simply not an effective way to modify behavior to desirable and permanent change: learning. A parent or a teacher who implements rewards rather than punishment will cause learning to be joyful and not fearful. The most readily apparent procedure for reward or punishment in a college is the grading system, but the system emphasizes the acquisition of grades for their own sake rather than for learning. In order to improve communications between student and teacher and to enhance learning, the college grading policy should be modified to eliminate the negative, punishing "D" and "F" grades.

3. *A Quotation*

Occasionally the words of someone else may be so striking and pertinent that you may wish to include the *quotation* in your introductory paragraph. This works especially well if the quotation relevant to your subject is by a well-known person.

> Hammurabi wrote in 2100 B.C., "If a man destroy the eye of another man, they shall destroy his eye." Some 3847 years later Voltaire wrote, "It is better to risk saving a guilty person than to condemn an innocent one." The first statement means that the punishment should fit the crime, but the second statement indicates that the punishment should not be irrevocable if future evidence indicates error. Under a jury system of criminal justice it always remains possible for mistakes in judgment to be made. Consequently, capital punishment, a sentence from which no reprieve is possible once it has been carried out, must be eliminated from civilized society.

4. *A Rhetorical Question*

Although you should generally avoid asking questions of any kind in your papers, sometimes beginning an introductory paragraph with a *rhetorical question* can be effective. Writers do not expect answers to rhetorical questions, but they do force readers to respond in particular ways with them.

> How long are Americans willing to allow millions of dollars of their tax money to be spent to subsidize a product that is deadly to the health of everyone? This product also costs additional millions to treat its victims and relieve its untold grief and suffering. Still more millions are spent to clean up after its use and to bury its dead. Although sounding like an exaggeration and an over-statement, the facts are plain; smoking is a heinous crime against one's self and society. Stiff laws that are effective and enforceable should be passed immediately to encourage the tobacco farmers to turn to useful crops, to end all encouragement for tobacco sale, and to prohibit tobacco use in any public gathering place.

**EXERCISE 2**

_____

Write an *introductory paragraph* in which you use **one** of the four techniques discussed in this lesson. (Choose any subject)

Subject Chosen: _____

Technique chosen: _____   **199**

Introductory Paragraph: _____

_____

_____

_____

_____

_____

_____

_____

_____

_____

_____

_____

_____

_____

_____

_____

_____

_____

_____

Have your work checked.

## LESSON THREE—Revising Your Introduction

When you have finished writing your paragraph, you are not yet finished with it. To submit a paragraph that has not been revised many times is tempting but foolish. After going to all the trouble of organizing and writing, it is ridiculous to turn in a paragraph that is not well thought out or error free. The process of **revision** requires you to reword everything that may be even slightly improved. You must check the *content, structure,* and *mechanics* of your written work as you edit and proofread.

### Revising Your Opening Sentence

The **opening sentence** is the first detail to be reviewed. It must be checked for interest and for its relationship to your thesis. You should seriously consider how you can best catch your reader's attention in the opening sentence. Notice the opening sentence of the paragraph about the gooney birds. Because the conflict appears improbable, the reader becomes involved in what is said about the defeat of the United States Navy by a flock of birds. Any of the following could also have served as a beginning sentence for that paragraph:

Who would believe that the United States Navy is being defeated by gooney birds?

or

The greatest navy in the world cannot defeat the gooney birds.

or

All the military might of the United States Navy is helpless against a comical but determined enemy: gooney birds.

The opening sentences above attract interest although each is different. The most obvious feature of each is that it is interesting and provocative.

In addition to creating interest, these opening sentences hint at the content of the thesis. You should note, however, that your beginning sentence can very easily lead the reader's attention astray. If it does so, your paper has a weak beginning and may be unsuccessful from the start.

*Examples*

(not related)     There are many beautiful birds in the islands in the middle of the Pacific Ocean.

(boring)          The Midway Islands are small islands in the middle of the Pacific Ocean.

(dull)            The Midway Islands are the home of the gooney birds.

(better)          The gooney birds and the United States Navy can both be found on the Midway Islands.

(best)            Two hundred and fifty thousand gooney birds have defeated the United States Navy for the past thirty years.

Every one of these sentences could be used as a beginning sentence for an introductory paragraph discussing the conflict between the gooneys and the Navy; however, the last would be most effective because it more accurately introduces the subject to be discussed.

Write *opening sentences* for each of the following thesis sentences. Make sure you compose interesting sentences that are not too close or too far from the thesis. (Remember, for a complete introductory paragraph three additional sentences would be needed between your opening sentence and your thesis.)

1. (*opening sentence*) _____

_____

_____

_____

(*thesis*) Hang-gliding is often dangerous if one is not alert for sudden shifts in the wind, for unfamiliar terrain, and for inexperienced operators.

2. (*opening sentence*) _____

_____

_____

_____

(*thesis*) By eliminating engine warm-up time, by avoiding "jack-rabbit" starts, and by traveling no faster than fifty-five miles per hour, everyone can help conserve rapidly dwindling automobile fuel supplies.

3. (*opening sentence*) _____

_____

_____

_____

(*thesis*) Since contemporary American voters seem to feel powerless to affect real change, few participate in the election process.

4. (*opening sentence*) _____

_____

_____

_____

(*thesis*) The bomb-laden train which exploded in Roseville, California, would have caused incredible loss of life if not for the early hour, the efficiency of railroad personnel, and the fast-acting disaster units.

Have your sentences checked.

## Irrelevant Sentences, Sentence Variety, and Transitions

Once you are certain that a relationship exists between your opening sentence and your thesis, turn your attention to the remaining sentences in the introductory paragraph. Three weaknesses may occur inside an introduction: **irrelevant material, lack of sentence variety,** and **poor transition.** Beginning writers always face the danger of including *irrelevant sentences.* A sentence is classified as irrelevant when it does not contribute to the topic under discussion. The following example illustrates this problem in an introductory paragraph:

> During the 1970's, a country that was seemingly satiated with sports gave new popularity to an old game: tennis. It was not as though there was not enough to watch on Sunday afternoons or that more high-paid, household-name stars were needed. However, the cult of personality and the great individual effort of tennis players was difficult to ignore, especially since the sport could be played equally well by men or women. *Some players were bad tempered and needed to be disciplined.* Although the match between Bobby Riggs and Billy Jean King was not great tennis, it went far in creating a public interest in tennis as a sport and in raising the status of women as players in all sports.

Notice how every sentence in the above paragraph except one comments on the growing popularity of tennis. That one italicized sentence which appears out of place, then, is not pertinent and must be removed; it belongs in some other composition.

As you check for unneeded sentences, also check for *sentence variety.* Too many sentences in the same paragraph that are similarly constructed will be dull for your reader. You should, therefore, change some sentences if you discover too many of any one type. As a general rule, more than two simple sentences in the same paragraph are too many; the same thing may also be said about compound sentences. Every paragraph should contain a mixture of simple, compound, and complex sentences, or your paper may sound boring. For example, the following introductory paragraph uses too many simple and compound sentences:

> (SS) In 1839 the slaves aboard the *Amistad* mutinied and killed the boat's captain. (CD) The ship had sailed from Havana, Cuba, and it was bound for another Cuban port. (SS) It carried a cargo of fifty-three slaves. (SS) The slaves attempted to get the crew to sail them back to Africa. (CD) The crew refused, and they sailed to New York. (SS) The boat was captured there. (SS) The ex-slaves were imprisoned. (CD) The *Amistad* mutiny was one of the very few successful mutinies by slaves, but it illustrates the strength of the slaves' hatred of slavery.

Although this paragraph communicates a large quantity of information, it fails to keep the reader involved because it moves haltingly. One of the reasons that the paragraph jerks along is that it contains too many simple and compound sentences.

Another cause for the halting nature of the above paragraph, however, is the absence of **transitions.** In Unit One, you worked with transitional words such as *however* and *therefore.* Notice how the same paragraph improves when sentence variations and transitions are worked into it:

> (SS)In 1839 the slaves aboard the *Amistad* mutinied and killed the boat's captain. (CD)The boat had sailed from Havana, Cuba, and it was bound for another Cuban port with a cargo of fifty-three slaves. (CX)When the mutinous slaves at-

tempted to get the crew to sail them back to Africa, **however**, the crew refused and sailed them to New York where the ship was captured and the slaves imprisoned. (CX)Although the *Amistad* mutiny was one of the very few successful mutinies by slaves, it illustrates the strength of the slaves' hatred of slavery.

This version of the *Amistad* paragraph is much improved because sentence patterns are varied and because a transition word is used. Revisions take time but must be made, for the smoothness of your composition often rests with your ability to use variety and transitions in your sentences.

The *sentence just before the thesis* deserves special attention, also. Coming as it does after the general background of the introduction, the second from the last sentence must move smoothly into the thesis by forming a **transitional bridge**. Across this bridge the ideas suggested in the introduction logically conclude with the thesis sentence. If the second from the last sentence does not form a smooth bridge into the thesis sentence, the introduction will seem to leap into the thesis with little apparent reason, and readers will be left wondering just how they arrived at the thesis so suddenly. Look back over the introductions in this unit noting the transitional bridges.

## 204 Proofreading for Mechanical Errors

In your final revision you must discover and eliminate all mechanical errors. To be sure, this is the easiest part of revising your paragraph; however, it requires you to reread your paragraph one word at a time. Using your dictionary frequently, you must discover every misspelled word, and every grammatical and punctuation error before you submit the final copy.

Revise the paragraph below by checking the following:
1. relationship between opening sentence and thesis
2. at least five sentences long
3. sentence variety
4. sentence transitions
5. irrelevant material
6. mechanics (spelling, punctuation, capitalization, grammar)

The small farm in America, is a thing of the past. The American ideal of being able to support one's family on a small plot of land, began when our country was first setled. This ideal; however, has changed during the last fifty years. The profits from a small farm has not increased during this time. The expenses have. The same problems may be found confronting the small businessman. At one time in America, the oldest son, could look forward to enheriting the family farm. Very few sons today inherit anything but the family debts. In fact all America seems to be in debt. In my opinion, today, the farmer who do not have a college education expensive machinry and extensive land holdings will almost certainly fail to support their family without supplimental income. Although large agribusiness is purchasing many farms.

**205**

Suggested revision on **page 212.**

Write an *introductory paragraph* on a subject of your choice. You may want to use a topic chosen in a previous exercise. For example, you could use the thesis you wrote for Section 5 of Exercise 8 in Unit 4, (page 131), or you could write an introductory paragraph to go with one of the body paragraphs you wrote in Unit Six.

Develop the introductory paragraph **carefully**, writing at least five sentences. Do your work on notebook paper and copy the final draft into this book. Then, after checking it over one last time, have your paragraph checked.

Have your work checked.

# LESSON FOUR—How to End It All

For many beginning writers the second most difficult task in writing is the **conclusion.** Getting started is hard, but after the words begin to flow, stopping them is often more difficult. Though difficult at first, once mastered, the concluding paragraph can be the most memorable for your reader in the whole composition.

The concluding paragraph is probably best understood as being the opposite of the introductory paragraph. Remember that the introductory paragraph *begins with a general statement*, then proceeds through a series of sentences that become successively more specific, and *finally ends with the thesis sentence*. In the concluding paragraph, the reverse is true. Begin your concluding paragraph with a **restatement of the thesis** of the composition. In restating the thesis, however, *do not repeat it word-for-word*. Rephrase the original statement so it will reassert the idea emphatically but not redundantly. Then, add three or four sentences that summarize the ideas developed in the composition, and, finally, add a relevant generalization that makes the paper end decisively, reinforcing its main ideas. Do not simply quit after your summary; another sentence is necessary to show relevance, universality, or applicability of your main idea. *Just as the opening sentence of the introduction must be both interesting and pertinent, the last sentence of the conclusion must communicate to the reader how what you have written is of lasting significance and relevance.* The first sentence and the last sentence of your composition help give your paper unity—a beginning and an end.

The concluding paragraph is your last chance to persuade the reader. Therefore, you should avoid the temptation to end upon a note of apology. *"I think . . ."* or *"In my opinion . . ."* are just as ineffective in the conclusion as they would have been in the beginning. Further, the concluding paragraph is not the place to bring in new ideas, new evidence, or added appeals. Remind your readers only of your most important ideas; refresh their memories. The content of the concluding paragraph is what readers take away with them, so take advantage of this last opportunity to demonstrate your assurance and conviction in what you have written.

## Review

In concluding compositions *at least five hundred words or longer*, devote a whole final paragraph to the *conclusion*. This last paragraph must leave a lasting impression on your readers. You want the readers to have the main points of the composition firmly fixed in their minds; therefore, restate the main points so that they are emphasized. Finally, end with a generalization that shows the lasting significance of your composition. In other words, the concluding paragraph should be one in which the whole composition is summarized.

## Examples

1

Population control is essential, and political pressures must be applied immediately. This goal is realistic. After being exposed and educated to the crisis, the world will bend. Society has always had individuals of vision who have dreamed and spoken of idealistic qualities of love, peace, beauty, and plenty. Now the vision is of simpler things: fresh air, clean water, food and the greatest gift of all, life itself. Population control is the bearer of this gift.

Every woman has the right to control her own reproductive life. Consequently, a woman should have the right to abort or not, just as she has the right to marry or not, or the right to use contraceptives or not. Many women have long fought for abortion law reform. However, women no longer want to reform anti-abortion laws; they want to abolish them altogether. They want to be free.

**Other Concluding Techniques**

1. For *very short compositions*, less than *five hundred* words, it is not usually necessary to have a concluding paragraph. Sometimes the *final sentence of the last body paragraph* will be sufficient for an effective conclusion.

   *Example*

   When others are present, any one bystander will assume that another observer is already taking action to end an emergency. Experiments have supported this theory. Every individual's reaction at the scene of an emergency is shaped by the action of others—and all too frequently by their inaction. A person can choose to realize the influence of a crowd, disregard it, and step forward to help. The alternative is apathy and, often, guilt.

The final point has impact; it can stand alone. As a result, this short composition needs no concluding paragraph.

2. Frequently, *two or three sentences at the end of a very short paper* that restate or summarize the main idea of the composition add an effective culmination.

   Even if the supersonic transport were not a "potential despoiler of the environment," the SST program is not one of national priority. The programs that deserve national attention and funding are those which can help alleviate some of the social injustices in the United States. No longer can technology be permitted to expand at the expense of so many for the benefit of so few.

3. Another effective technique is to conclude with a *quotation* that emphasizes the main ideas of the composition. (Make sure, however, that it is apt and to the point.)

   The prime function of the American system of government is to protect the populace from the righteous. The central democratic idea is that the majority of the people will save themselves. The only hope is that the majority can remain less righteous and more unsure of what is right. As the late Supreme Court Justice Learned Hand once said, "The spirit of liberty is a spirit which is not too sure it is right."

**208**

   Be certain to *avoid writing conclusions that introduce new ideas*. Any new idea at the end of a composition will leave readers dissatisfied. They will wonder why the writer chose to include it without development. In general, it detracts from the other ideas, the ones that were developed.

*Example*

    The brief career of the *Glomar Explorer* is but one example of a highly sophisticated and potent international intelligence gathering system. Granted, the surface publicity indicated that Project Jennifer was a failure, but an efficient information gathering network cannot publicly herald each new success. The raising of a Soviet submarine intact, complete with thermal-nuclear weapons, enabled American military scientists to ascertain the level of Russian technology. *After dismantling the Soviet Foxbat airplane, flown into Japan by a pilot wishing political asylum, American technicians learned that the plane, while an effective combat weapon, was not nearly as advanced as had been generally supposed.* Putting this new knowledge to work for America may eventually save millions of lives. The future of the world necessitates an effective, well trained, and adequately financed American intelligence community. No price can be too high for freedom.

One final word of caution when writing conclusions: do not equivocate. In other words, do not leave your readers in doubt as to where you stand. There will be doubt if the ending is in question. Readers do not want an idea tossed back to them for concluding answers. They are reading for those answers, so do not end with questions or equivocal statements that ask the reader to investigate the problem further or to decide for himself.

**209**

Write a **concluding paragraph** for the following composition outline.

**Opening sentence**

The world's oldest profession has, for centuries, been the unjustified target of the would-be guardians of the public's morals.

**Thesis sentence**

Although it would certainly be an economic bonanza for the state, the legalization of prostitution would also permit prostitutes to engage in free enterprise without harassment, restore long denied civil liberties to clients, and free the police to concentrate upon serious crime.

**Topic sentence #1**

The economic tradition of America has been the freedom to purchase and sell whatever one wishes without interference, subject only to *reasonable* safeguards for the public.

**Topic sentence #2**

Individuals are different; consequently, they should be able to seek their fortunes, choose their hobbies, and take their pleasures based upon their personal preferences and ethics without unwarranted interference.

**Topic sentence #3**

At present, untold numbers of valuable hours of police effort are expended in the pursuit, entrapment, and conviction of individuals who have committed victimless crimes such as prostitution.

_____

_____

_____

_____

_____

_____

_____

_____

_____

_____

_____

_____

_____

_____

_____

_____

_____

_____

_____

_____

_____

_____

_____

_____

_____

_____

## EXERCISE 7

Write a **concluding paragraph** to fit with an introductory or body paragraph written for a previous exercise, or, if you prefer, write one on a different topic.

_____

_____

_____

_____

_____

**211**

_____

_____

_____

_____

_____

_____

_____

_____

_____

_____

_____

_____

_____

_____

_____

_____

Have your work checked.

## Suggested Revision

The paragraph below has been revised. Your paragraph should have the same changes. However, since some additional variations in these changes are possible, you should discuss all differences with your instructor or a tutor. Each correction is underlined.

The small farm in America is a thing of the past. The American ideal of being able to support one's family on a small plot of land began when the country was first settled. This ideal, however, has changed during the last fifty years. The profits from a small farm have not increased during this time, but the expenses have. (The same problems may be found confronting the small businessman. Omit) At one time in America, the oldest son could look forward to inheriting the farm; however, very few sons today inherit anything but the family debts. (In fact, all America seems to be in debt. Omit) (In my opinion, Omit) Today the farmer who does not have a college education, expensive machinery, and extensive land holdings will almost certainly fail to support his family without supplemental income. (Although large agribusiness is purchasing many farms. Omit)

# UNIT EIGHT
## *The Complete Composition*

### *Objectives*

After completing this unit, you will be able to

1. label the *opening sentence, thesis, topic sentences, primary support,* and *secondary support* in a complete composition.
2. follow the basic conventions of expository writing.
3. identify the various *paragraph strategies* when used in full-length papers.
4. choose appropriate and interesting *general subjects* upon which to write.
5. divide a subject into its various topics.
6. select a manageable *topic* for development into a composition.
7. *limit the topic* so that the paper will maintain its focus.
8. develop effectively *divided* and *undivided* thesis sentences.
9. write *thesis-topic sentence outlines* which are adequate for development into compositions of assigned lengths.
10. write the *first draft* of a 500-1,000 word *expository paper.*
11. *revise* the first draft of an expository paper to insure proper paragraph development, transitions, and sentence construction.
12. produce the finished copy of an expository composition.
13. use proper *con-pro* development for an argumentative paper.
14. write argumentative papers structured to use *idea-by-idea* and *paragraph-by-paragraph* development.
15. write a 500-1,000 word *argumentative composition.*

**213**

# 8

Learning sentence structure and paragraph strategies is important because such skills are the foundation of effective compositions. At this point you should have mastered those skills and be ready to begin the development of your first complete composition. The subjects you wrote on in Units Four, Five, Six, and Seven are perfectly acceptable in this unit; in fact, since you have already given thought to them, you should save considerable time and effort by using them. Occasionally, you will even be able to use paragraphs written for earlier exercises as you develop complete compositions for this unit, after you have revised them, of course, so they will fit smoothly into the total paper.

But whatever topic you write on and however you go about the development of it, be sure you do your best. The skills that you learn in *Writer's Workshop* culminate in Unit Eight; these are the skills that will help you in future courses as well as your career.

## LESSON ONE—Review

Think back to everything covered in the first seven units. One step at a time, you worked through many aspects of writing compositions. You began by composing simple sentences, proceeded through introductory, body, and concluding paragraphs. Your study and writing so far, however, has been concerned only with parts of compositions rather than the whole paper. Unit Eight, by contrast, considers the total composition. Consider carefully the following typical 500-1,000 word paper. After reading the paper, answer the questions which follow it. (You may need to briefly review parts of Units Three through Seven to answer the questions.)

### KID'S LIB

(1) *One of the most profound changes emerging from the twentieth century is the sexual revolution.* (2) One result of this revolution is that people are becoming increasingly aware of the dangers of restricting the life choices of individuals to narrowly defined sex-roles. (3) The contemporary view is that

individuals and ultimately society can reach highest fulfillment by encouraging the development of unique talents and aptitudes of people rather than arbitrarily assigning traditional roles based on an individual's sex. (4) But what happens too often is that the institutions of society, through archaic practices, perpetuate these outmoded role models. (5) Public education is a prime offender, as demonstrated by the content of some of its textbooks. (6) The **Janet and Mark** series currently in use in many states as a reading primer is one example of the way archaic sex-role models are perpetuated. (7) *The characterizations of the adults and children in the stories offer hopelessly narrow stereotypes bearing little relationship to the beginning readers' life experiences because the Janet and Mark series offers a "fuddy-duddy" view of how a good, decent family should live in middle America.*

(8) *Mother is the good, old-fashioned homebody.* Her hair is short and plain in a 30's style, and she always wears drab house dresses of below-the-knee length. (9) Sometimes she wears an apron to be sure to keep flour and sugar off her nice clean dress. (10) Her creative energies seem to reach fever pitch when she bakes and dusts. (11) Occasionally she is shown returning to the nest from her sole outside activity, grocery shopping. (12) Mother never seems to tire or become irritable even though most school children know from experience that shopping, cleaning, chauffering, and cooking are tiring jobs and that their own mothers get irritable and tired. (13) Janet and Mark's mother always looks calm, placid, and slightly amused.

(14) *Male roles are hopelessly stereotyped, too.* (15) Dad is a real "Nowhere Man." (16) He has barbershop-trimmed hair and usually wears a white shirt and tie. (17) He is most often pictured arriving home from work in a grey suit and hat. (18) What he does all day is never explored, presumably because his activities are beyond the interest or mental capacities of his off-spring. (19) He expends his creative energies fixing toys, reading the newspaper, and smoking a pipe. (20) Dad is always calm and banally smiling, especially when he takes his leadership position as head of the family, assuming control of the car on the proverbial Sunday afternoon drives on that big family highlight, a trip to the farm to see Grandma and Grandpa. (21) The old folks are greyed, plump versions of Mother and Dad. (22) Their activities are similarly structured; Grandpa tends to the tractor and animals, and Grandma churns butter.

(23) *"Normal" children's roles and activities are dramatized through the behavior of the protagonists, Janet and Mark.* (24) Their activities are determined more on the basis of sex than personal inclination or interest. (25) Janet and her friends (all girls) wear dresses and hair ribbons. (26) In the one instance where a girl is shown in pants, she is playing in a field, so her transgression of the rule is forgivable. (27) Like Dad, Mark and his friends (all boys) have short, clean-cut looking hair and wear standard-Sears clothes, invariably neat and clean. (28) Mark and company are allowed more adventure in their activities than the girls. (29) A model relationship between the sexes is gently suggested when Mark climbs a tree to rescue Janet's kitten. (30) One of the few examples of cooperation between the boys and girls occurs when Janet agrees to teach Mark to roller skate if he will teach her to ride a bicycle. (31) Even their cooperation has a sexist bias. (32) The implication here is that boys ride bikes (symbolizing independence—a prototype of supposed male mechanical interest and aptitude) sooner than girls. (33) But then the little lady has wheels of her own, even if smaller and more restrictive in function.

(34) *One story in particular reveals the sexist bias of Janet and Mark.* (35) Mark is given an astronaut costume complete with NASA-style blue jumpsuit and plastic bubble helmet. (36) He runs to show Janet his costume. (37) She responds by inviting him into her child-sized playhouse. (38) Inside she pours him pretend tea and shows him around the place. (39) Janet has a charming little

bedroom and kitchen setup, complete with pretend baby (doll) in a cute little cradle. (40) She even has sweet miniature curtains on the little window. (41) They sit on the bed and talk about their playthings. (42) And so that leaves the couple happy—Mark literally equipped to "trip-out" to outer space, and Janet doing her best to keep him right there at home with her little seduction scene.

(43) *The stilted vision of adult life in the* **Janet and Mark** *series could adversely influence children's attitudes, especially as one of their earliest educational experiences.* (44) Restricting options before children are even aware of the available choices discourages the development of self-actualized adults. (45) If the goal of compulsory education is to produce aware, mature persons capable of making meaningful life choices and judgements, this stifling of human potential cannot be healthy for children or society as a whole. (46) Stimulating, imaginative textbooks will challenge children's creativity right from the start.

## EXERCISE 1

**Matching**. From the list of terms on the right, select the letter of the term which describes each sentence designated by the numbers in parentheses on the left. (Answers on page 241)

1.  (1) _____
2.  (7) _____
3.  (8) _____
4.  (14) _____
5.  (15) _____
6.  (16) _____
7.  (17) _____
8.  (18) _____
9.  (19) _____
10. (20) _____
11. (21) _____
12. (22) _____
13. (23) _____
14. (34) _____
15. (43) _____

a. thesis sentence

b. secondary support sentence

c. opening sentence

d. topic sentence

e. primary support sentence

f. summary sentence

# LESSON TWO—The Structure of a Whole Composition

Writing that explains is called **expository** writing. An *expository paper* is normally a complete composition that explains a concept, an event, a movement, or a process in depth and requires the writer to be very knowledgeable about the topic because of this depth. Consequently, since your instructors are actually asking you to explain how much you know when they ask you to write a composition for a course, the majority of the papers you write will be expository. Although your assignment will vary from instructor-to-instructor and class-to-class, the basic structure and purpose of all such writing will be essentially the same.

Because your main purpose in expository writing is to *explain*, and since your papers reflect what you know, it follows that you should make every effort to express yourself as clearly and completely as possible. Researching, reading, discussing, and reviewing your notes will help you write a better expository paper, of course, but you must first understand the conventions and structure of the paper. The following conventions are generally recommended by instructors:

### Guidelines for Expository Writing

1. Write a strong thesis statement.
2. Use third person only (first person acceptable for anecdotes).
3. Never copy someone else's words unless you give credit to your source.
4. Do **not** begin a paragraph with the pronoun "it."
5. Make sure every paragraph contains at least *five* sentences.

These are only a few of the most obvious writing conventions; you will add to the list as you become a more accomplished writer.

With experience, you will also gain a deeper understanding of effective organization for your papers. You will find, for instance, that all papers are similar: a collection of paragraphs which support a central idea or thesis. After you truly understand the organizational structure of compositions, you will realize that writing is not difficult; all you need are some basic skills and some imaginative ideas.

Consider the following diagram.

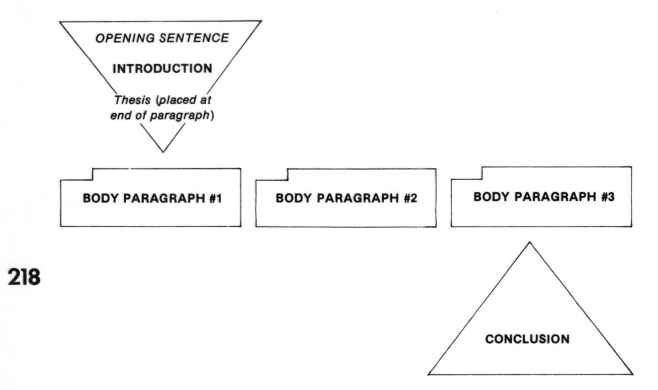

**218**

Notice that the diagram shows schematically the framework for a typical five-paragraph composition. You have seen many of these diagrams in this book, but now you will actually develop a five-paragraph paper. Remember first, though, what you learned about the various paragraph strategies. The following expository strategies were introduced in Units Five and Six:

### Paragraph Strategies

1. Illustration
2. Definition
3. Comparison/Contrast
4. Analysis
   a. Process
   b. Structural
   c. Cause-and-Effect

You have already written one or more paragraphs using each strategy; however, you may find that you need to review how each pattern works before reading further. The following exercise will enable you to assess your ability to recognize each paragraph type.

## EXERCISE 2

As you read the paper, identify the particular strategy used in each paragraph on the line beside it. (Write the words *Introduction* or *Conclusion* before all paragraphs in the introduction and conclusion portions of the paper.) Answers on page 241.

### Roots for 25 Million Americans

Many have long believed that American slaves enjoyed being slaves, that they were actually happy with their lives. This ridiculous belief grew out of the mistaken idea that Africa was populated by cannibalistic savages who had no religion. To justify their participation in this barbaric slavery and to lessen the guilt in their own minds, slave traders and plantation owners perpetrated stories about supposed savagery in Africa and fabricated stories which illustrated what they called the low mental ability of the African people. This nonsense was, unfortunately, believed by millions of ignorant Americans, white and black alike.

_____(1) Only a few well-educated people knew that these stories were false, and their knowledge was rarely passed along to common people. When it was passed along at all, it was written in scholarly language that the average American would not even attempt to read. The deliberate lies by those who profited from slavery together with this ignorance produced an environment in which white and black Americans did not respect those of African descent. With the publication of *Roots*, a book by Alex Haley, which can be read and understood by anyone, this lack of respect should rapidly disappear. *Roots* clearly shows that Africans came from a very respectable society, that slaves did not like slavery, and that the slavery which existed in Africa was entirely different from that in America.

219

Too few people understand what American slavery was; the lies told two centuries ago still influence people's thinking. Slavery was, in reality, an inhuman practice that deliberately destroyed the identity of those it victimized. Those who enslaved others recognized that human beings who did not know who they were would not cause as much trouble as those who were proud of themselves and their heritage. For this reason, slaves were not allowed to learn to read or write; to keep their African customs, religion, and language; or to meet and talk with other Africans. Slavery was, furthermore, the only way for the Southern society to survive economically. Slave labor was the cheapest way of getting fields cleared, crops planted and harvested, and heavy chores done without inconvenience to the farmer. Little background is required for a person to realize that the "Old South" was never able to rise again after the Civil War primarily because there were no slaves to work the fields.

_____(2)

*Roots* begins with an intense examination of life in the back country African village where one slave was captured. The family's religion, the Moslem faith, was a dominating factor in their lives; it gave purpose and order to everything. This religion discouraged tobacco and alcoholic drink, so lung diseases and alcoholism were unknown. In addition, the book shows how important village life was to these peace-loving, agricultural people. Every member of the village respected all other villagers; no one was looked down upon because he or she was a slave or poor. Even the old people in the African society were a part of the smoothly functioning village. Elders were advisors, teachers, and historians, and their opinions were listened to intently. Tradition, like religion and respect, gave meaning to the Africans' lives. Men cultivated the cotton crops while women cultivated the rice. Women took care of the youngest children while men did the hunting. Young boys guarded the goat herd while middle aged boys guarded the village. These roles had been a part of the African way of life for centuries, and every member of the community knew at all times exactly what he or she was expected to do. The astute reader, knowing something of what American slave culture was like, rapidly realizes that the society from which the slaves came was not at all similar to the descriptions of it which are commonly held.

_____(3)

Although Alex Haley does an outstanding job of describing a slave family's overall experiences, it is the African ancestor, Kunta Kinte, who best shows how the slaves felt about slavery. Taken from his native village when he was seventeen, be began fighting against slavery immediately. Kunta fought the slavers, in spite of overwhelming odds, and only quit fighting when rendered senseless. His fighting back continued for years. It is Kunta Kinte's reaction to life as a slave, however, that most clearly gives the reader an idea of how slaves felt. So keen was his dislike of slavery that he repeatedly ran away. Even though he knew that he would be beaten savagely when recaptured, he never failed to run when the opportunity presented itself; this is exactly how most slaves felt about the practice. Even after the professional slave-catchers cut off half of Kunta's foot with an axe and prevented any further escape attempts, he never accepted the role as property offered by plantation owners. Even while pretending to accept his role as a slave, he secretly taught his daughter of her African heritage; by doing so, he let her know that she had roots, that she was someone.

_____(4)

Haley's *Roots* points out, as many others have done, that slavery also existed in Africa, but Haley goes one step further and shows how totally different it was from American slavery. Unlike American slaves, African slaves were not considered property; rather, they were respected members of the community. Slaves took part in village life and even intermarried with other members of the village. Furthermore, African slaves had guaranteed rights. They could not be beaten, regardless of the importance of their masters. The master of an African slave could not sell his slave without permission of the slave. And most important, all slaves in Africa were assured of the right to buy their freedom whenever they so desired. In America, people became slaves for life whenever they were born with black skin; in Africa, people became slaves for a limited period when their village was defeated in battle or when crop failures resulted in famine and they needed someone to provide them with food.

_____(5)

**220**

————————(6) In a very unique way, *Roots* tells about slavery and the African people who were victimized by it. But the book does more than just tell about slavery; it also presents black Americans as a people with a heritage of which anyone could be proud. This one characteristic of the book may be the most important because all people need to know from where they came. Black and white Americans alike might very well realize after reading *Roots* that the society to which Africans were brought as slaves was far less civilized than the one left behind.

The preceding paper may be used as a model for the future structural analysis papers you write. Approximately 1,000 words in length, it is a fairly typical assignment in many classes. Even for a paper with an assigned length of 500-1,000 words, this is not at all too long; it is usually better to be too long than too short. Because the sample paper above examines or analyzes the book *Roots*, it would be classified as an analysis composition. But you should observe that the author of the paper has chosen to use various paragraph types in the body. You will rarely write a paper in which every body paragraph employs the same strategy. Here the overall approach used is *analysis* because the paper examines or analyzes the book *Roots*, but the author of the paper has chosen to combine various strategies to accomplish the general effect desired.

## LESSON THREE—The Expository Paper

Every paper begins with an assignment, whether made by an instructor or by you. *How easily you get from assignment to completed paper depends on how well prepared you are, how difficult the assignment is, and how you go about developing that paper.* Of those three variables, the one you have the most control over is how you proceed with your paper's development. If you begin in an orderly, deliberate fashion, the final paper will not only be easier to produce, but it will also result in a better composition. Every paper you write should develop through an *eight-step process* between assignment and the final product.

**Eight Steps to a Good Paper**

1. Decide upon a subject.
2. Identify topic possibilities.
3. Select the topic right for you.
4. Limit the topic.
5. Develop the topic into a thesis.
6. Outline the paper.
7. Write a first copy and revise.
8. Prepare a final copy.

Although it is possible to develop a paper without following each of the steps above after you are an experienced writer, you should not attempt to do so now. Perhaps you might think it a bother to follow each step while developing your paper, but the confidence of knowing that the paper you submit is done correctly will be adequate repayment for following each step carefully.

In the remainder of this lesson, you will develop a 500-1,000 word paper, following each of the eight steps previously listed. You will be given a model upon which to base your first six steps. To save yourself time, you may select a subject you wrote on in Units Four, Five, Six, and Seven. Even though the paragraphs you have already developed will require some revision, you can revise much faster than you can create entirely new paragraphs. Moreover, because you have already given considerable thought to that subject as you wrote those paragraphs, you are probably better prepared to write on that subject than on any other.

Step #8—Final copy

Step #7—First copy

Step #6—Outline paper

Step #5—Develop thesis

Step #4—Limit Topic

Step #3—Select topic

Step #2—Identify topic possibilities

Step #1—General subject selection

## Step #1—Deciding Upon a Subject

Deciding upon a *general subject* can be easy or hard, depending on circumstances. If your instructor assigns a paper and the subject, Step #1 is done for you. More commonly, however, an instructor will assign a paper and give you a choice of general subjects upon which to write. In such a case, Step #1 will be slightly more difficult. Regardless of which of the positions you find yourself in when it comes time to select a subject, two considerations should guide your choice: what subject do you know the most about, and what subject will most likely be received well by your instructor? You will, of course, spend less time doing research if you select a subject you already know something about. Suitability should also be considered. If your instructor is interested in reading about history and photography, it would only be logical to assume that a paper about riding motorcycles in motocross races would not be interesting—unless that subject were offered as a possibility when the paper was assigned.

### Sample Assignment

Write a 500-1,000 word paper on *one* of the following subjects.

1. Computer crime
2. Endangered species
3. Unequal taxation

**222**

Selecting **the best** subject should not be a drawn-out process. Decide in a few minutes which is best and then stay with your choice. Do **not** switch back and forth. When you decide upon a particular subject, write it down. Do not just keep it in your mind. To illustrate how a paper should be developed, the general subject of *endangered species* has been followed through Step #1 to Step #6; you will be asked to develop a subject through the same steps.

Step #1—Endangered species

## EXERCISE 3

Select a *general subject* from Units Four, Five, Six, or Seven, and write it in the blank below.

Step #1 _____

## Step #2—Identify Topic Possibilities

Just as the subject should be selected quickly, there is no reason to spend more than a few minutes considering *topic possibilities*, **provided** that you know something about the subject already. If the subject is familiar to you already, simply write down a list of three or more possible topics under the general subject you chose in Step #1. When you do not know very much about the assigned subject, go to the library and research the subject briefly, using the card catalog or the *Reader's Guide to Periodical Literature*. Step #2 should be, in reality, no more than a process whereby you narrow down your subject to a list of specific topics.

The following is a list of possible topics appropriate to the subject of *endangered species*.

Step #1—Endangered species
Step #2—Possible topics

1. Harp seal          4. wolf
2. dolphin            5. polar bear
3. whale              6. condor

## EXERCISE 4

Select a list of at least three *possible topics* dealing with the subject you identified in Step #1.

Step #2

1. _____
2. _____
3. _____
4. _____
5. _____
6. _____

**223**

### Step #3—Select the Topic Right for You

After the topics are listed, you can study them briefly. Consider which topic you feel the most strongly about; that topic is often the one you should write about. If you write on a topic you care nothing about, your paper will very likely become an exhausting chore for you and a boring paper for your reader. A paper written on a topic which appeals to you, however, can be stimulating for you and your reader. But remember that time matters, so spend no more time than absolutely necessary selecting the *topic right for you.*

The topic chosen for illustration is the Harp seal topic. (The topic chosen should be written down clearly to avoid confusion later.)

Step #1—Endangered species

Step #2—1. Harp seal      4. wolf
         2. dolphin      5. polar bear
         3. whale        6. condor

Step #3—Harp seal

---

**EXERCISE 5**

---

Select the *topic* about which you intend to write.

Step #3 (topic) _____

### Step #4—Limit the Topic

*Limiting the topic* takes considerably more thought than Step #1, #2, and #3. In fact, the more thought you give to limiting your topic, the easier it will be to write your thesis. Because your topic in Step #3 will invariably be very general, you must consciously narrow it until it only deals with the aspect or aspects of the topic upon which you intend to write. At this point many papers begin to go astray, so you should have your progress checked before you go on to Step #5 if you are at all unsure. When you have completed the limiting of your topic, it must be perfectly clear about what you intend to write.

Step #1—Endangered species

Step #2—1. Harp seal      4. wolf
         2. dolphin      5. polar bear
         3. whale        6. condor

Step #3—Harp seal

Step #4—The brutal slaughter of baby Harp seals

**224**

**EXERCISE 6**

---

Write your *limited topic.*

Step #4 (limited topic) _____

## Step #5—Develop the Topic into a Thesis

Writing a *thesis* is undoubtedly the most important step; if your thesis does not work, your paper will never succeed. Reread the section on the development of an effective thesis statement in Unit Four if you are not sure about thesis development. Remember that the thesis controls virtually your entire paper; therefore, you should proceed deliberately to develop the very best thesis statement you possibly can.

You may find it most convenient to divide your thesis, but that is not absolutely necessary as the following examples illustrate:

Divided thesis—

Because baby Harp seals are being slaughtered without restraint, the mating patterns of the flocks are being altered, the size of the flocks themselves is shrinking, and the species is in danger of extinction.

Undivided thesis—

The unrestrained slaughter of the baby Harp seals will cause traumatic changes of the species unless immediate steps are taken.

Which thesis will produce the best composition depends on the writer. For some people, the *divided thesis* is best because it outlines the entire paper. For others the *undivided thesis* provides freedom to be more spontaneous. You should be guided by whether or not you feel the need of the structure offered by the divided thesis.

*Developing your thesis should not be difficult if you approach it logically.* Possibly the best technique is to begin by asking yourself a *question*. In the case of the sample limited topic in Step #4, you might merely ask, ''What about the brutal slaughter of baby Harp seals?'' The answer to this question would be the thesis in rough form. For instance, you might answer that''The slaughter of baby Harp seals is unnecessary and needlessly cruel and must cease.'' Before going on to the next step, however, you should refine the thesis again and again until it reflects exactly the paper you wish to write.

Step #5—thesis statement should look like those following:

Question:      What about the brutal slaughter of baby Harp seals?

Rough Thesis:  The slaughter of baby Harp seals is unnecessary and needlessly cruel and must cease.

Final Thesis:  Because baby Harp seals are being cruelly slaughtered without restraint, the mating patterns of the flocks are being altered, the size of the flocks is shrinking, and the species is in danger of extinction.

## EXERCISE 7

Develop your *thesis*.

Question: _____

_____

_____

**225**

Rough Thesis: _____

_____

_____

_____

Final Thesis: _____

_____

_____

_____

Have your work checked.

## Step #6—Outline the Paper

A *thesis-topic sentence outline* is composed of an opening sentence, a thesis statement which gives direction to the entire paper, a topic sentence for each body paragraph, and a summary statement for the concluding paragraph. You should begin developing your outline by writing the thesis statement; this will give the remainder of your outline the proper direction. The length of your paper will dictate the numer of topic sentences in your outline. If the assignment is to write a five-hundred word paper, you will probably need three body paragraphs and, therefore, three topic sentences. However, if you are assigned a one-thousand word paper, you will need about six topic sentences. Plan ahead before writing an outline to avoid trouble later. Assume that a good paragraph will have 100-150 words in it, (at least *five* sentences) and construct your outline accordingly.

After you have copied your thesis statement from the last exercise, develop a topic sentence for each body paragraph. Remember that each topic sentence must precisely support the thesis; make the relationship very clear so the final paper will be effective. Then when you are convinced that you have written those sentences as carefully as you possibly can, write a summary or restatement sentence for the beginning of your concluding paragraph. The concluding paragraph should summarize every one of the major ideas you have covered in the body of the paper. Finally, if you have not already done so, write an opening sentence that will attract your reader's attention at the same time that it introduces the subject about which you intend to write. Many writers compose the opening sentence last because it is easier after writing the remainder of the outline.

To illustrate the procedure for developing an outline, see the Harp seal outline below.

**226**

*Opening sentence:* Babies are being killed in the most brutal ways imaginable.

*Thesis sentence:* Because baby Harp seals are being slaughtered without restraint, the mating patterns of the flocks are being altered, the size of the flocks is shrinking, and the species is in danger of extinction.

*Topic sentence #1:* Scientists have noticed that as the size of the flocks shrink, the female seals are pressured into mating at a younger age.

*Topic sentence #2:* Although the Harp seals are still numerous in some areas, the total population of these beautiful creatures is merely a fraction of what it once was.

*Topic sentence #3:* As incredible as it sounds, the rapidly decreasing size of the flocks and the mechanization of their slaughter make the extinction of the species almost certain.

*Summary sentence:* Because the valuable pelts of these beautiful baby Harp seals are so highly prized, hunters and governments have furiously defended the slaughter as they continue their bloody business.

The thesis-topic sentence outline above would probably be adequate for a 500-750 word paper. As you work the exercise below, be certain you develop an obvious relationship between your thesis and the topic sentences. (Use the thesis sentence you developed in Exercise 7.)

**EXERCISE 8**

Develop a *thesis-topic sentence* outline for a 500-1,000 word paper.

*Opening sentence:* _____

_____

_____

_____

*Thesis sentence:* _____

_____

_____

*Topic sentence #1:* _____

_____

_____

*Topic sentence #2:* _____

**227**

_____

_____

*Topic sentence #3:* _____

_____

_____

_____

*Summary sentence:* _____

_____

_____

_____

Have your outline checked.

### Step #7—Writing a First Copy of Your Paper

#### *Expanding the Outline: Two Methods*

Expanding your outline into the first copy of a paper should be easy. If you have paragraphs in Units Four, Five, or Six which could be used in this paper, use them; of course, you will almost certainly need to revise them so they will fit into the paper you are developing, but the revision should not be difficult. How a person actually writes the paper differs from writer to writer and from paper to paper. There are, however, two primary approaches to writing papers. The most common developmental technique is for the writer to *begin with the opening sentence of the paper in the outline and proceed as rapidly as possible with the writing until the last paragraph has been completed.* If you elect this technique, do not become bogged down with the introductory paragraph. Whenever your first paragraph appears awkward and you cannot decide how to make any more progress, simply go on to the next paragraph; you can always return to complete the unfinished paragraph later. The second approach to writing a paper is to *begin with the first* **body** *paragraph and write each following paragraph as rapidly as possible.* When all body paragraphs and the conclusion have been completed, the writer then goes back and writes the introductory paragraph. You should try both of these approaches before deciding which is best for you.

#### *Writing Conditions*

Write your paper under carefully controlled conditions. First, set aside a large block of time for your writing so you can write the entire first copy without interruption. One continuous writing period will produce a paper that has a pleasing smoothness to it. If you do some of the writing one day, more of it on a second day, and complete it on a third day, a rough and uneven paper may be the result. The second condition **228** upon which you should insist is a quiet atmosphere in which to write. If your living quarters cannot provide you with such conditions, plan to go to some isolated corner of the library during the quiet afternoon hours. No distractions should be permitted. Above all, though, the writing of the paper should be done rapidly. Write without excessive concern for proper punctuation, spelling, sentence structure, and other mechanics. In the first copy you should only be concerned with putting your ideas on paper in the order they appear on your outline.

**When writing your first copy:**

1. Set aside a single block of time for writing.
2. Create a good writing environment.
3. Write rapidly.

### *Revising the First Copy—Second Copy*

Once you have completed the first copy, you are ready to *revise*. Surprisingly, this second copy normally takes about the same length of time as the writing of the first copy. If you spend two hours producing the first copy, you will probably need at least two hours to revise it. You should plan to write the first copy one day and do your revision another day, if time will permit such a relaxed approach. This time lapse will allow you to return to the paper with fresh attitude and eyes, thereby allowing you to discover and cure weak sentences and paragraphs.

### *Paragraph Revision*

When you have gone through your first copy one sentence at a time, you are ready for what might be the most important phase of the revision: the *paragraph revision*. Every paragraph, of course, must have at least five sentences in it; moreover, good sentence variety must be immediately apparent. In addition, previous units have stressed the need for transitions, interrupters, and conjunctive adverbs to smooth out the paragraphs. Equally important, however, are transitions between paragraphs. Every paragraph must be smoothly and effectively connected to the paragraph before and after it. Smooth, effective transitions between paragraphs are a must; when paragraphs jump roughly from one idea to the next your reader will be unable to follow the development of ideas.

### *Smooth Transitions*

The most comfortable transitions for you to use at this point are those you learned in previous units. Words such as *however, therefore, moreover, consequently,* and *nevertheless* are common transitions which you should already have mastered. When you properly use one of them in the beginning sentence of a paragraph, two paragraphs join smoothly almost every time. When you use a technique called "repetition of key word," you repeat an important word or concept from the end of one paragraph in the first sentence of the following paragraph. Read the following paragraphs and observe how skillfully the writer has tied his ideas together. The connecting transition, which ties

paragraph one with paragraph two, is italicized. Later, the italics identify the repetition of the key word which connects paragraphs two and three. (This is only a portion of a much longer paper.)

In 1964, a Canadian film team, Artek Films of Montreal, happened to be on the ice while the annual seal hunt was taking place. Unknowing, the hunters produced for the film team quite a display of their handy work. The white, silky-furred baby seals called "whitecoats" were the objects of the hunt, but because of the close proximity of the seals, slaughter is a better description. Boasting of "seven different methods" of killing the seals, the hunters quickly went about their task. Time was valuable because after the first week the pups moult, developing a coarser, shorter coat of less market value. In their haste, many hunters began to skin the pups before they were dead; several of their "seven methods" only injured instead of killed. (In 1966 the Canadian Government reacted and forbade the killing of the animals by any method other than clubbing with a specified hardwood bat.) The small baby seals were often killed in front of their mothers, and their bodies left on the ice since they have no market value as meat. Forlorn-looking mother seals mourned for days over the frozen carcasses of their babies. Subsequent pictures and disclosures by the film team shocked the world.

*Consequently*, the Canadian Federation of Humane Societies asked Mr. Brian Davies to attend the hunt as an SPCA observer. During the next five years accompanied by a veternarian, photographers, and various newspaper and magazine reporters, Davies substantiated in great detail the sequence of events portrayed in the Artek film. In view of all the damaging evidence of the savage brutality to the seals, how can the slaughter of the baby seals be allowed to continue? The divisions are strictly drawn between officials concerned over local economy, fishermen who want to preserve their industry, furriers who insist on the right to harvest a valuable marine product, and wildlife environmentalist and humane organizations who demand a permanent end to the *hunt*.

Seal *hunting* has been a factor in local culture for many years. In a lengthy *National Geographic* article in July, 1929, Captain Robert A. Bartlett recreates the excitement and danger of that year's *hunt*. He compares the opening day to opening of deer season in the United States. Captain Bartlett was a fifth generation seal hunter and boastfully tells of the year 700,000 seals were caught. In 1934 another Newfoundland sealing captain, Abram Kean, earned the Order of the British Empire by bringing in his millionth seal. Disregarding the commercial huntsmen, such as Captain Bartlett and Captain Abram, the annual returns for the local landsmen through the years have been very low. Most hunters are only casually employed during the winter, and the hunt represents a change from winter boredom. In recent years, their hunting profits have been as low as $39 and as high as $102 compared to the 1929 figure of an average $60 per year.

The paragraphs above from a paper on seal hunting excesses illustrate how paragraphs can be smoothly joined. As you read the following paper, notice how the paragraphs are joined; *underline* the transitions and repeated key words. (Answers on page 241)

### Participatory Democracy Lost, Apathy Gained

An epidemic is spreading throughout the nation that is a greater threat than the plagues of the Dark Ages. The name of the disease is "apathy." Thirty-eight people in New York contracted "apathy" several years ago while viewing the murder of Catherine Genovese. They watched for nearly half an hour and did not attempt to halt or report the crime. Examples of this lack of concern toward society, though perhaps not as drastic as the Genovese murder, are becoming frequent occurrences. Obviously, some factor must be contributing to this attitude that permeates the nation. The American system of government has alienated the people, creating in them a lack of responsibility toward civic involvement. Since the days of ancient Greece, democracy has, out of necessity, taken a different form, causing problems, one of which is social apathy.

The structure of Athenian democracy stressed participation of the citizens. The Council of Five Hundred, or popular assembly, conducted the city-state's affairs. The five hundred members were chosen by lot from the body of citizens. Any citizen was eligible. A second institution in Athenian government was the citizen's jury. It consisted of six thousand jurors. Because the jurors were paid, the poor could serve. Altogether, one-fifth of the population of Athens held an office, and the majority of the remaining people took an active part in the community affairs as private citizens.

The massive involvement of the Athenian citizenry promoted a sense of obligation toward the state and community. Young men of eighteen upon receiving citizenship were proud to spend two years in the military service. Many citizens made generous contributions to the government in addition to taxes. Others provided funds for the entertainment of the community. One man spent fourteen thousand dollars, a great amount of money in those times, for public feasts and theatricals.

This type of involvement exhibited in Athens is rarely seen in America today. Young men do not feel proud to serve in the military forces. This fact is proved by the number of draft evaders during the Vietnam War. People do not make contributions to the government willingly. Some, Joan Baez, for example, refused for several years to pay taxes. And if a citizen does do something for the community, it is simply an act of promotional advertising. This is the condition of the American society. A look at the system of government shows why.

Certain conditions in the American society have made it necessary to produce a democracy different from the type of democracy practiced in Athens. The boundaries of citizenship have been broadened in America to include women and foreigners. The population has increased many-fold as compared to that in ancient Athens. The complexity of modern American society leaves people with less free time than Athenians had. The percentage of educated and informed citizens has dropped from that of Athens because the percentage of uneducated people who are citizens has risen in America. All these factors inhibit consistent interaction of the majority of Americans in government. A more practical, indirect system has been activated—representative democracy. This form of government dictates that the people elect representatives who have the time and education to handle all government affairs.

**231**

Unfortunately, shifting responsibility for the nation from the people to a selected few has alienated many Americans. Not participating in national or community administration has destroyed their sense of obligation toward society. This pattern of alienation has persisted. Americans feel too far removed from their representatives and the vast bureaucracy they control. Many Americans feel deeply frustrated because they are unable to control the actions of government and are dismayed at the extent to which corrupt, unethical, and immoral practices prevail. But they feel so helpless in remedying these evils through their representatives that they grow confused and cynical and decide not to become involved. Eventually they do not even care. The lack of civic involvement in America has increased, resulting in a decreased immunity and a subsequent outbreak in social apathy.

## Proofreading for Errors

After your paragraphs flow smoothly, you should examine each sentence for mechanical errors. Errors in spelling, capitalization, and punctuation are easily discovered if you consciously look for them. More serious errors such as fragments and comma faults may be harder to see, but they too can be picked out when you seriously search for them one sentence at a time. Mistakes in sentences, however, must be removed before you prepare your final copy.

## EXERCISE 10

Write your *first copy* of a 500-1,000 word paper. Do your work on notebook paper. Write on one side only.

## EXERCISE 11

*Review the first copy of your paper.* Your paper's grade will depend on how well it achieves the following list of qualities. The paper should have

1. a strong, effective thesis sentence.
2. clear topic sentences.
3. five or more sentences in every paragraph.
4. the first word of every paragraph indented.
5. interesting opening sentence.
6. precise summary sentence and effective conclusion.
7. adequate sentence variety and smooth transitions.
8. no first or second person.
9. no awkward or grammatically incorrect sentences.
10. no fragments.
11. no comma faults.
12. no spelling, punctuation, or capitalization errors.

**232**

## Step #8—Preparing the Final Copy

Your *final copy* should be especially neat and carefully prepared, but it should also be easy to write. Once your editing and proofreading process is complete, little work remains except for re-copying your work. However, you should never be unwilling to revise a paragraph—or your entire paper—if you find problems when making that final copy.

## Format For Final Draft

1. Write in ink, skipping every other line, or type, double spacing.
2. In the upper left-hand corner of page one, write your name, the course title, meeting time, instructor's name, and the date the paper is to be submitted.
3. Write or type only on one side of each page.
4. Center the title of your paper two inches from the top. If you are writing in ink, capitalize the first letter of each word, except prepositions, articles, and conjunctions that are not the first word of the title. If you are typing, capitalize all letters in the title.
5. Indent at the beginning of each new paragraph; do *not* leave an extra-wide space between paragraphs.
6. Leave ample but not excessive margins—left, right, and bottom.
7. Beginning with page two, number each page in the upper right-hand corner.
8. Last-minute corrections can be made by neatly drawing a single line through the portion to be revised or corrected and printing the correction above the crossed-out portion. Additions should be inserted above a caret mark, (∧).
9. Proof-read your composition carefully just before you hand it in. If many corrections or extensive revisions are made, re-write or retype the page or the entire paper.

**EXERCISE 12**

---

Prepare and submit your *final copy* in ink (it may be typed). When you hand in your final copy, be sure you attach the first copy to the back of it.

## LESSON FOUR—The Argumentative Paper

In this lesson you will learn how to recognize and how to write **argumentative compositions**. The type of argumentative paper most commonly written differs from the **expository paper** most obviously in the body. The body paragraphs in an argumentative composition should *debate the con's and pro's of your thesis*. In the body of an argumentative composition do not merely explain with a list of reasons why your thesis should be believed. Instead, argue back and forth, admitting that arguments against your case do exist, but always turning around to refute the opposing points. The order in which you admit and refute opposing arguments is important. Always acknowledge a point of opposition before you reason against it. In other words, always end up on your side. Do not weaken your position by following a statement supporting your thesis with a statement raising objections to that statement. Briefly and honestly summarize the particular objection you are discussing; then persuasively reason against it. If you have ever had any training in sales, you will probably think it odd that you are supposed to admit objections to your case, but in academic writing, which purports to be objective and scholarly, con-pro arguments are traditional and, therefore, expected.

**233**

### Thesis

When you write an argument, do not forget how important your **thesis** becomes. Ideally, the *thesis of an argument should be a precise sentence which outlines or foreshadows the rest of the paper*. Furthermore, *the thesis sentence should be opinion-*

*ated and debatable.* Here are some examples of thesis sentences written for arguments: (Remember, these are not necessarily true statements. They are assertions that the authors will attempt to defend.)

1. Although the courts are established to uphold the rights of the citizens granted in the Constitution, they have become increasingly negligent of their primary duty, interpreting the law, and as a result have caused the law itself to lose its stability and certainty.

2. Because research studies have indicated that the effects of marijuana are no worse than those of alcohol and since no cause-and-effect relationship between marijuana and harder drugs has been established, the use of "grass" should be legalized with the same restrictions that apply to the sale and use of alcohol.

3. By winning the election in 1976, President Carter re-established the cherished American belief that any citizen can reach the country's highest office without being part of a Washington political machine.

4. In spite of its beauty and insightfulness, *Children of Dune* is not as prophetic a book as *Dune*, the author's first book about the residents of Arrakis.

**Transitions for Arguments**

To write clearly structured arguments, you must make ample use of certain *transitional words and phrases* traditionally employed as roadsigns signaling the direction the argument is to take. Thus, not only should you use these transitions frequently in the middle of your arguments, or wherever they are needed, you should also use them properly, according to their traditional functions, to avoid misleading your reader. For example, *But*, with a capital B, placed at the beginning of a sentence, is a traditional signal that a writer is turning on a point of opposition he has just admitted. If you use **But** to introduce a *con* point, you might send a false signal to the reader, making him think that you were embarking on a discussion on the *pro* side, in other words, on your side. Try to memorize this short list of transitional words and phrases, or at least consult the list repeatedly until you become experienced at writing arguments:

| CON | PRO | CONCLUSION |
| --- | --- | --- |
| of course | but | therefore |
| no doubt | however | thus |
| doubtless | yet | so |
| to be sure | on the contrary | and so |
| granted | not at all | hence |
| granted that | surely | consequently |
| certainly | no | finally |
| perhaps | still | on the whole |
| conceivably | nevertheless | all in all |
| although | notwithstanding | in other words |
| though | furthermore | in short |
| whereas | indeed | |

**234**

**Switching From Con to Pro Within the Paragraph**

The first of the following compositions demonstrates how easily a con-pro argument can be structured. While reading "Space Exploration," notice how carefully the paper is organized and how effortlessly the writer moves from one idea to the next. From beginning to end the composition is very persuasive. Observe how each "con" is answered with a point that supports the thesis.

## Space Exploration

INTRO

A heated debate recently erupted in the staid halls of Congress. Some Congressmen, it seems, were certain funds being proposed for the space effort could be better spent to eradicate poverty. They asserted that the expenditure for space research was an extravagance that the country could not afford. If these same Congressmen would put aside constitutional grandstanding and party posturing, they would quickly see the essential value of a space program. A review of the arguments for and against the space effort quickly shows it to be a major force for eradicating poverty in America.

THESIS

CON

The first argument used against space exploration is that it draws off funds that could be used to build low-cost housing for the poor. There can be no question about the need to rid America of its slums. The last census showed that over half of the people who live in American cities have inadequate housing. But the developmental work done on Skylab I and II has made modular construction possible. The revolutionary breakthrough in prefabricated housing promises to make it possible for low cost quality construction. Of course, those opposed to the space program could argue that Rohr Corporation, the originator of the system, could have developed the process on their own, or developmental money, they argue, could have easily been sent to Rohr by HUD as by NASA. On the contrary, the legislation proposed by these same Congressmen shows they support only those programs designed to provide immediate construction, not research. Therefore, American tax dollars could be spent perpetuating a system that has failed to provide housing. Modular housing probably would never have been developed. Consequently, money spent in continuing the space program offers continued research and development in new and better ways to provide housing.

PRO

CON

PRO

CON

Jobs are another chief concern of those opposed to the exploration of space. Their position is that money could be better spent providing jobs for thousands of people. They speak of programs similar to those used by the Roosevelt Administration during the Depression. Granted, such programs, if they would be accepted by the public, would provide stop-gap employment. But is that a real solution to the problem of unemployment? Developments in space science have provided and will continue to provide millions of people with jobs. Teflon, an ablative material used to coat re-entry nose cones, created a whole new industry employing thousands. The same is true for transistors, computers, digital readout equipment and many, many other developments of space research. All in all, there can be no comparison between the few jobs offered in a program of stop-gap employment and the fruition of new industries from the developments of space science. In short, the exploration of space has provided and will continue to provide employment for millions of Americans.

PRO

CON

Opponents of the space program use the old argument that money would be better spent in research and development of new food sources right here on earth. Undoubtedly, the need is here, and it should have first priority. Yet there have been some smashing scientific breakthroughs that clearly show that a denial of food research in the space program would be a mistake. A classic example is the discovery in the preservation of food. Scientists at The University of California, Davis, recently perfected a way to preserve and store meat and fruit for indefinite periods. This was a direct result of deep space research. Now, for the first time in human history, bad harvest years and disease-ravaged cattle herds need not create soaring

PRO

**235**

prices and empty tables. On the whole, the miniscule amount of money spent on food research in the space program has paid for itself many times over.

CON

Another of the major arguments used by the opponents of space exploration expenditures is that space science is creating an educational and cultural gap of ever-widening proportions in America. They state that in the future there will be the super-educated and the uneducated. To keep funding the space program, they argue, is to perpetuate a misguided national infatuation with science and engineering. Perhaps there has been too much emphasis on science and technology in recent years. Conceivably, there could be a gap as they describe it. Perhaps the poor see themselves being left behind as the scientists speed off to distant horizons. There can be no argument against the right of all Americans to self-realization. Certainly no program should be funded that denies this potential to any American.

PRO

But surely, those who voice their objection to the space program on such grounds owe it to themselves and their constituents to do some research. Education for the common man has never been more opportune than today. Thanks to such developments as multimedia devices, teaching machines, video tapes, computerized records systems, and micro-record storage, the means to an education is within the grasp of all with the mental ability to avail themselves of it. All of these developments can be directly linked to American efforts to solve the mysteries of space. Rather than widening that gap, space research has placed a bridge across it that millions can use to take themselves from the state of fear and confusion to the territory of knowledge and understanding. That bridge is there. They need only to avail themselves of it.

CONCL

Clearly, two positions exist on the issue. One, however, would appear to be much more valid than the other. Let those congressmen who would cut off funds for the space program do some homework. Let them put aside their politicking and give the space exploration program a fair and impartial appraisal. When they do, they will quickly discover it to be a major force in providing housing, food, jobs, and education, in short, a force moving to eradicate poverty in this country.

The student paper you have just read clearly illustrates one way *con-pro* development can be used in an argumentative paper. Each paragraph begins with a *con* statement which argues **against** the position taken by the thesis. After the *con* sentence is supported so that it is clear, a *pro* sentence answers that *con* and supports the position taken by the thesis. Notice that every *con* sentence is answered in the same paragraph; this technique effectively keeps the reader from mistakenly thinking that the opponent's argument is correct.

### Paragraph-by-Paragraph

**236**

Many writers, regardless of how well they understand the developmental technique demonstrated above, prefer a second commonly employed technique. The second most frequently used argumentative organization is the *paragraph-by-paragraph development*. The writer using such an approach develops one *con* paragraph immediately following the thesis; this paragraph explores that *con* position in depth. When the point has been clearly made, the writer develops a *pro* paragraph which argues against the *con* paragraph; this switching back and forth normally occurs many times in a single paper. Both of these *con-pro* developments are equally effective. The one you choose to use in your own writing depends upon your preference.

As you read the second argumentative paper, "Mineral King," pay special attention to the author's skillful use of transitional words and phrases. They have been italicized to allow you to pick them out easily.

## Mineral King

INTRO

A war over the use of the national forests rages in the United States. Conservationists are arguing that land should remain untouched and left for future generations to appreciate. The Forest Service and private recreational industries, on the other hand, debate that the public, having greater leisure time, needs more developed recreational areas. One such conflict is over the Mineral King Basin in California. Walt Disney Enterprises with the cooperation of the Forest Service has proposed to turn the valley into a ski and tourist resort. Carrying through this proposal would be tragic. Because the development of Mineral King would doom the beautiful valley to urban blight and ecological destruction, the project should be abandoned.

THESIS

CON

*To be sure*, Mineral King is ideally located and would become a popular tourist attraction. It lies halfway between Los Angeles and San Francisco, the two largest population centers in California. The basin could be easily reached by the state's freeways and a proposed twenty-six mile road, which would replace the present dirt road into the Mineral King Valley. Due to the location and accessibility the suggested daily capacity is fourteen thousand people, and it is estimated that there would be 2,500,000 visitors annually.

PRO

The influx of people into the basin, *however*, would definitely cause problems similar to those Yosemite National Park is experiencing 150 miles away. Yosemite has been plagued by smog, crime, noise pollution, and trouble with sewage disposal, problems all directly attributed to the park's overwhelming popularity. Yosemite Valley is several times larger than Mineral King Basin; yet, the daily use projected for Mineral King would produce three times the concentration of people found at Yosemite on a busy day. Therefore, it is foreseeable that Mineral King would be doomed to even greater problems than those being experienced at Yosemite.

CON

*Granted*, the United States Forest Service favors the proposed resort and was, in fact, the initial instigator. In February, 1965, the Forest Service issued a prospectus outlining a development estimated to cost three million dollars. They received six qualified bids and chose the Disney proposal for a $35,000,000 development. The proposed resort would include a ten-story parking structure, a 1,030-room hotel complex, a convention center, a theater, an equestrian center, indoor and outdoor swimming pools, and an ice-skating rink; in addition, there would be a half-dozen ski lifts. The job of the Forest Service is to protect the nation's forests and to see that any development is in the public's interest. Thus, the Forest Service assumed it was in the public interest to develop Mineral King and that the bigger the development the better for the public. With this in mind, they accepted Disney's proposal.

PRO

*Nevertheless*, the Forest Service ignored the possibility of damage to Mineral King's ecology. The Forest Service's responsibility is to protect America's national forests; yet, it conducted no investigation to determine the ecological impact such a development would have on the basin. If such a study were made, it would certainly point out the tragic effects of such a proposal. The trees that hold the shallow layer of soil on the slopes would be cut to make room for the ski lifts. The soil would then be washed down the mountains and into the river; the result would be siltation, a situation which is deadly to fish. In addition, growth of vegetation would be hampered. The

**237**

growing season in the Mineral King Basin is short; once destroyed by heavy foot and horse travel, the vegetation would never grow back. The various species of wild life that now make the valley their summer home because of the abundant forage would be forced to move.

CONCL

Therefore, the development of Mineral King Basin into a resort should be abandoned. The basin should be kept free of smog, crime, and noise pollution; its delicate ecology should be protected against erosion and loss of flora and fauna. Mineral King should be left in its wilderness state, not ruined by the type of recreational development found in Yosemite that has resulted in city-related and ecological problems.

**EXERCISE 13**

Argumentative papers are prepared exactly like expository papers: one step at a time. Deliberately develop the *outline* for a 500-1,000 word paper, from subject to outline in the space provided.

Step #1—general subject chosen _____

Step #2—topic possibilities _____

_____

_____

_____

Step #3—topic selected _____

_____

Step #4—limited topic _____

_____

Step #5—thesis sentence _____

_____

_____

_____

238 Step #6—thesis-topic sentence outline

Opening sentence _____

_____

_____

Thesis sentence _____

_____

_____

_____

_____

Topic sentence #1 _____

_____

_____

_____

Topic sentence #2 _____

_____

_____

_____

Topic sentence #3 _____

_____

_____

_____

Topic sentence #4 _____

_____

_____

_____

Topic sentence #5 _____

_____

_____

_____

Topic sentence #6 _____

_____

_____

_____

_____

Summary sentence _____

_____

_____

_____

_____

Note! You may not need to develop all of the topic sentences indicated above. The number you develop, however, will almost certainly determine the length of your final paper, so you should plan for at least three. Before going on to the next exercise, have Exercise 13 checked.

**EXERCISE 14**

Following the outline in Exercise 13 carefully, write the *first copy* for a 500-1,000 word paper. Do your work on notebook paper; have it checked before doing the next exercise.

**EXERCISE 15**

Develop your *revised copy* into the final draft and submit it to your instructor.

When your instructor has graded and returned your Exercise 15 paper, you have successfully completed the text and should be ready to take the final test. After you have reviewed Unit Eight, ask to take the final test. Good luck and **congratulations!**

# ANSWERS FOR UNIT EIGHT EXERCISES

## Exercise 1 (page 217)

1. c
2. a
3. d
4. d
5. e
6. b
7. e
8. b
9. e
10. e
11. e
12. b
13. d
14. d
15. f

## Exercise 2 (page 219)

| | |
|---|---|
| *introduction* | paragraph #1 |
| *definition* | paragraph #2 |
| *analysis* | paragraph #3 |
| *illustration* | *paragraph #4* |
| *contrast* | paragraph #5 |
| *conclusion* | paragraph #6 |

## Exercise 9 (pages 231-232)

### Participatory Democracy Lost, Apathy Gained

An epidemic is spreading throughout the nation that is a greater threat than the plagues of the Dark Ages. The name of the disease is "apathy." Thirty-eight people in New York contracted "apathy" several years ago while viewing the murder of Catherine Genovese. They watched for nearly half an hour and did not attempt to halt or report the crime. Examples of this lack of concern toward society, though perhaps not as drastic as the Genovese murder, are becoming frequent occurrences. Obviously, some factor must be contributing to this attitude of uninvolvement that permeates the nation. That factor is the system of government. The American system of government has alienated the people, creating in them a lack of responsibility toward civic involvement. Since the days of ancient Greece, *democracy* has, out of necessity, taken a different form, causing problems, one of which is social apathy.

The structure of Athenian *democracy* stressed participation of the citizens. The Council of Five Hundred, or popular assembly, conducted the city-state's affairs. The five hundred members were chosen by lot from the body of citizens. Any citizen was eligible. A second institution in Athenian government was the citizen's jury. It consisted of six thousand jurors. Because the jurors were paid, the poor could serve. Altogether, one-fifth of the population of *Athens* held an office, and the majority of the remaining people took an active part in the community affairs as private *citizens*.

**241**

The massive involvement of the *Athenian citizenry* promoted a sense of obligation toward the state and community. Young men of eighteen upon receiving citizenship were proud to spend two years in the military service. Many citizens made generous contributions to the government in addition to taxes. Others provided funds for entertainment of the community. *One man spent fourteen thousand dollars,* a great amount of money in those times, *for public feasts and theatricals.*

This type of *involvement* exhibited in Athens is rarely seen in America today. Young men do not feel proud to serve in the military forces. This fact is proved by the number of draft evaders during the Vietnam War. People do not make contributions to the government willingly. Some, Joan Baez, for example, refuse to pay taxes. And if a citizen does do something for the community, it is simply an act of promotional advertising. This is the condition of the *American society.* A look at the system of government shows why.

Certain conditions in the *American society* have made it necessary to produce a democracy different from the type of democracy practiced in Athens. The boundaries of citizenship have been broadened in America to include women and foreigners. The population has increased many-fold as compared to that in ancient Athens. The complexity of modern American society leaves people with less free time than Athenians had. The percentage of educated and informed citizens has dropped from that of Athens because the percentage of uneducated people who are citizens has risen in America. All of these factors inhibit consistent interaction of the majority of Americans in government. A more practical, indirect system has been activated—representative democracy. This form of government dictates that the *people elect representatives* who have the time and education to handle all government affairs.

Unfortunately, *shifting responsibility* for the nation from the people to a selected few has alienated many Americans. Not participating in national or community administration has destroyed their sense of obligation toward society. This pattern of alienation has persisted. Americans feel too far removed from their representatives and the vast bureaucracy they control. Many Americans feel deeply frustrated because they are unable to control the actions of government and are dismayed at the extent to which corrupt, unethical, and immoral practices prevail. But they feel so helpless in remedying these evils through their representatives that they grow confused and cynical and decide not to become involved. Eventually they do not even care. The lack of civic involvement in America has increased, resulting in a decreased immunity and a subsequent outbreak in social apathy.

242

# *Index*

244

**245**

*Notes*

# REVISION SYMBOLS

| | |
|---|---|
| Ab | Abbreviation is faulty |
| Agr | Agreement is faulty |
| Awk | Awkward expression |
| Cap | Capitalization needed |
| CS | Comma splice |
| Dev | Development inadequate in this paragraph |
| DM | Dangling modifier |
| Frag | Fragment |
| Gr | Grammar error |
| Irr | Irrelevant material |
| Jarg | Jargon |
| LC | Lower case letter |
| Mis | Misleading statement |
| MM | Misplaced modifier |
| MS | Manuscript form error |
| Paral | Parallelism is faulty |
| Pn | Punctuation |
| Pron | Pronoun |
| Rep | Repetition |
| Ref | Reference of pronoun unclear |
| RO | Run-on sentence |
| S | Sentence fault |
| Sp | Spelling |
| Tense | Tense of verb inappropriate |
| Trans | Transition is ineffective |
| Trite | Trite phrase |
| ? | Unclear statement |
| Var | Variety lacking in sentence structure |
| Wordy | Wordy sentence |